China and Vietnam: The Roots of Conflict

A publication of the
Institute of East Asian Studies
University of California
Berkeley, California 94720

The Indochina Monograph series is the newest of the several publications series sponsored by the Institute of East Asian Studies in conjunction with its constituent units. The others include the China Research Monograph series, whose first title appeared in 1967, the Korea Research Monograph series, the Japan Research Monograph series, and the Research Papers and Policy Studies series. The Institute sponsors also a Faculty Reprint series.

Correspondence may be sent to:
Ms. Joanne Sandstrom, Editor
Institute of East Asian Studies
University of California
Berkeley, California 94720

INDOCHINA RESEARCH MONOGRAPH   1

INSTITUTE OF EAST ASIAN STUDIES
UNIVERSITY OF CALIFORNIA • BERKELEY

China and Vietnam: The Roots of Conflict

WILLIAM J. DUIKER

Although the Institute of East Asian Studies is responsible for the selection and acceptance of manuscripts in this series, responsibility for the opinions expressed and for the accuracy of statements rests with their authors.

Copyright © 1986 by the Regents of the University of California
All rights reserved
ISBN 0-912966-89-0
Library of Congress Catalog Card Number 86-81534
Printed in the United States of America

Contents

List of Abbreviations vi
Introduction vii
    I.   The Legacy of History 1
   II. China and the Vietnamese Struggle for Independence 8
 III. Beijing, Hanoi, and the Second Indochina War 35
 IV. Descent into Conflict 63
   V. The Struggle for Cambodia 95
 VI. The Road to Reconciliation 116
Selected Bibliography 126
Index 132

Abbreviations

AFP	Air France Press
ASEAN	Association of Southeast Asian Nations
CCP	Chinese Communist Party
CKC	*Cuoc khang chien chong my cuu nuoc 1954–1975: nhung su kien quan su* [The anti-U.S. resistance war for national salvation, 1954–1975: military events]
CMEA	Council for Mutual Economic Assistance
DRV	Democratic Republic of Vietnam
FBIS	Foreign Broadcast Information Service
FEER	*Far Eastern Economic Review*
FUNK	National United Front for Kampuchea
ICP	Indochinese Communist Party
JPRS	Joint Publications Research Service
KCP	Kampuchean Communist Party
KNUFNS	Kampuchean National United Front for National Salvation
KPRP	Kampuchean People's Revolutionary Party
NCLS	*Nghien Cuu Lich Su* [Historical research]
NCNA	New China News Agency
PAVN	People's Army of Vietnam
PLA	People's Liberation Army
PMUN	Permanent Mission to the United Nations
PRC	People's Republic of China
PRK	People's Republic of Kampuchea
SEATO	Southeast Asia Treaty Organization
SRV	Socialist Republic of Vietnam
TCP	Thai Communist Party
VCP	Vietnamese Communist Party
VNA	Vietnamese News Agency
VWP	Vietnamese Workers' Party

Introduction

The Sino-Vietnamese conflict of 1979 burst like a clap of thunder on a stunned world. For a generation, China and Vietnam had been wartime allies and ideological comrades-in-arms, possessing a common commitment to world revolution and a shared hostility to the imperialist camp led by the United States. During the Vietnam War China had provided, by its own estimate, at least $10 billion in support of the Vietnamese struggle for reunification. While that support may not have been decisive in the achievement of total victory in 1975, by any calculation it was instrumental in bringing about the eventual withdrawal of U.S. troops and the unification of Vietnam under communist rule. In gratitude, Vietnamese President Ho Chi Minh once declared that the relationship between the Chinese and the Vietnamese revolution was made up of "a thousand ties of gratitude, attachment, and love, a glorious friendship that will last forever."

Today, a decade after the fall of Saigon, China and Vietnam are locked in a bitter dispute, marked by territorial disagreements, divergent views about the world situation, and a serious rivalry over influence in Southeast Asia. Official statements emanating from both capitals show that the dispute has deepseated historical roots, and had festered under the surface during several decades of surface cooperation. By all indications, the rupture is unlikely to be resolved in the near future, and threatens to become one of the enduring features on the regional landscape in East and Southeast Asia.

The Sino-Vietnamese dispute raises a number of interesting issues for Asian specialists and students of international politics. What are its origins? Must they be sought in the past, in the tangled historical relationship that has existed between the two peoples for over two millenia? Or should the split be viewed primarily in terms of such contemporary issues as ideology, power politics, and territorial agreements? What is the role of the Cold War in the conflict? Was the Sino-Vietnamese conflict that broke out in 1979 an outgrowth of local rivalries, or a "proxy war" in which regional participants were acting as surrogates for larger powers on the world scene? What were the specific causes of the Vietnamese invasion of Cambodia in 1978 and the Chinese attack on Vietnam in the following year? Can the dispute be resolved, or has it become irrevocably imbedded in the global Cold War among the Great Powers? Such questions are of more than mere academic interest. They go to the heart of the dispute, and they represent the key to a possible resolution of the conflict.

This study will trace the roots of the Sino-Vietnamese conflict in the hope of providing insight into such questions. Because of the limitations of space, it will concentrate on the sources of the dispute rather than on the complex rivalry that followed the outbreak of open conflict in early 1979. I have chosen to adopt the chronological approach partly because, as a historian, I am comfortable with such a methodology, but also because such an approach will illustrate my conviction of the importance of historical factors in the emergence of the dispute.

Research on such a subject represents a considerable challenge to the scholar. Because neither China nor Vietnam is an "open society" in terms of the dissemination of information, one is dependent upon limited official sources, "managed" news, and the official tendency to rewrite history. Such practices, of course, are present to some degree in almost all societies, but they are more prevalent in relatively closed systems such as China and Vietnam. Documentary evidence is limited, and government archives are not open to Western scholars.

Fortunately, the researcher is not totally devoid of information from within China and Vietnam. Reports by foreign scholars and journalists are fairly numerous, and the translation services of the Foreign Broadcast Information Service (FBIS) and the Joint Publications Research Service (JPRS) provide rapid and accurate publication of newspaper and journal articles and radio broadcasts in the two countries. I am also personally grateful for the opportunity to undertake short visits to the two countries to interview specialists at the Institute for International Studies in Beijing and at the Institute of International Relations and the Ho Chi Minh Museum in Hanoi, as well as the Ministry of Foreign Affairs in Phnom Penh. I also benefited from interviews with officials at the Embassy of the People's Republic of

China in Washington, D.C., and the Vietnamese Mission to the United Nations in New York City.

A number of people have helped me in various ways in the preparation of this manuscript. I am grateful to Tao Bingwei and Ye Xin of the Institute for International Studies in Beijing for granting me an extended interview on the subject of Sino-Vietnamese relations in August 1985 and to Yang Guanqun of the Chinese Embassy in Washington, D.C., for his assistance in arranging the visit. I would like to thank the Institute of International Relations in Hanoi for extending to me an invitation to visit Vietnam and to Nguyen Dang Quang and other members of the staff of the Vietnamese Mission at the United nations for help in obtaining a visa. Deputy Director Nguyen Quang Du and other staff members at the institute were tireless in sharing with me their views on various issues related to Vietnamese foreign policy. Mr. Nguyen Dinh Vinh kindly took time out from his other duties at the institute to accompany me on a three-day trip to Ho Chi Minh's native province of Nghe Tinh. I also benefited from discussions with Director Ha Huy Giap and Nguyen Huy Hoan at the Ho Chi Minh Museum and with Director Van Tao at the Institute of History. Vo Dong Giang, Minister of State for Foreign Affairs of the SRV, kindly accorded me an extended interview on the current state of Sino-Vietnamese relations and other regional issues. In Phnom Penh, Deputy Foreign Minister Kong Korn and other officials at the Ministry of Foreign Affairs generously made themselves available for discussions on the current situation in Cambodia.

Thanks are also due to Richard Bridle, Georges Boudarel, Nayan Chanda, Arnfinn Jorgenson-Dahl, Lyman Miller, David Marr, Douglas Pike, Robert Porter, Leo Suryadinata, Jim Taylor, Carlyle Thayer, Bill Turley, and Lacy Wright for sending me their own articles on the subject or sharing their ideas with me in person. Joe Zasloff was a stimulating traveling companion during my recent visit to Vietnam and the PRK, and I benefited greatly from his views on the experience. Lew Stern and his wife, Mary, warmly extended their hospitality during my stopover in Bangkok. I am also grateful to Mona Perchonok for her typing and editorial assistance. My visit to Vietnam and China was funded by grants from the Institute for the Arts and Humanistic Studies and the College Fund for Research of the

College of the Liberal Arts at The Pennsylvania State University. None of the above, of course, is responsible for the views expressed herein, which are my own.

As always, I am especially grateful to my family for its understanding and support: to my mother, Jeanne S. Duiker; to my sister, Mary; to my daughters, Laura and Claire; and finally to my wife, Yvonne, who takes charge of family responsibilities without complaint so that her husband can spend his time banging at the typewriter.

William J. Duiker is professor of East Asian history at Pennsylvania State University. A former U.S. foreign service officer, he is the author of several books and articles on Vietnam, including *Vietnam since the Fall of Saigon* (Ohio University Press, 1985).

I
The Legacy of History

It is in the nature of the historian to seek the sources of human conflict in the past. Behavior between nations, as between individuals, is often motivated by a complex amalgam of emotions, assumptions, and expectations, many of which are a product of experience. Without an understanding of such factors, it is difficult if not impossible to grasp the ultimate causes of the conflict itself.

This generalization is particularly true in the case of the recent conflict between China and Vietnam. The historical relationship between the two peoples is one of unusual complexity. Throughout history, the political and cultural ties between the two societies have been close. For nearly one thousand years, Vietnam was an integral part of China; and even after independence was restored in the tenth century, Vietnamese rulers frequently accepted what is often described as a "tributary relationship" with China and often turned to their powerful northern neighbor in time of need. Yet, for the Vietnamese, respect has often been tinged with fear and suspicion. For more than two millenia, China represented the primary threat to the independence and national identity of the Vietnamese people, and it is not too much to say that the Vietnamese nation has been formed, in considerable measure, in the crucible of its historic resistance to Chinese conquest and assimilation.

In essence, then, the historical relationship between China and Vietnam has had an almost symbiotic character. It is a long one, extending back several centuries prior to the beginning of the Christian era. The ancestors of the present-day Vietnamese first appeared as one of a number of scattered peoples (generally known to the Chinese as the *Yueh*—in Vietnamese, *Viet*) living along the southeastern coast of the Asian continent from the Yangtze estuary in the north to the Red River Delta in the south.

Most of these peoples were later absorbed into the expanding Chinese empire and are today considered a part of the majority Han race living in modern China.

The furthest south of the *Yueh* settlements, situated in the marshy delta of the Red River Delta in what is today known as North Vietnam, were the *Lac* people, the immediate ancestors of the modern-day Vietnamese. Although ethnically and linguistically related to the other so-called Yueh peoples along the southeastern coast of China, the Lac gradually forged a distinctive culture that sometime during the second millennium B.C. took political shape in the form of the kingdom of Van Lang. Recent archaeological evidence suggests that Lac civilization was relatively advanced. Not only did the Lac apparently master the techniques of bronze casting at an early date, they were among the first peoples in the area to make extensive use of irrigation in the cultivation of wet rice.[1]

The political implications of such evidence are considerable. Previously, many modern scholars had accepted the views of generations of Chinese historians, who contended that the Lac, like their Yueh counterparts to the north, were a relatively primitive people whose absorption into the Chinese empire introduced them to advanced civilization. Modern archeology is beginning to discover, however, that the Lac, like many of the Yueh peoples living in southern China, were not significantly less advanced than the allegedly superior cultures from the north who brought them under Chinese rule in the late first millennium B.C. As for the Lac themselves, contemporary Vietnamese historians are quick to point out that the growing evidence about the kingdom of Van Lang demonstrates the indigenous origins of Vietnamese civilization.[2]

---

[1] For recent articles on the development of rice culture and bronzecasting in ancient Vietnam, see the June and July 1984 issues of *Vietnam Courier*. The best source on ancient Vietnam in English is Keith W. Taylor's *The Birth of Vietnam* (Berkeley and Los Angeles: University of California Press, 1983).

[2] An authoritative statement of this view is the article by Truong Chinh, "The long struggle to defend our national culture," *Tap Chi Cong San* [Communist review], no. 3 (March 1979). This article has been translated in Joint Publications Research Service (hereafter JPRS) 73,511. For an interesting overview of Vietnamese historiography on this issue, see Sophie Quinn-Judge, "Tradition and myth of the elusive Vietnamese Camelot," *Far Eastern Economic Review* (hereafter *FEER*), March 14, 1985. For a Chinese view of early relations

Whatever the degree of distinctiveness of the state of Van Lang, it did not escape the fate of the other Yueh settlements along the coast to the north. The rise of Lac culture coincided with a gradual southward expansion of the Chinese civilization which culminated in the absorption of much of the Yueh territory and the formation of the first centralized empire of the Qin (Ch'in) in the late third century B.C. While the Qin empire lasted less than a generation, it was succeeded by the more durable dynasty of the Han, which consolidated the power of the Qin and built upon its imperial foundations.

Under the Han, the southward expansion of Chinese civilization continued. During the first century B.C., the Lac were conquered and assimilated into the Chinese empire. The process was gradual. At first, Chinese administrators were content to rule the area indirectly through the local landed aristocracy, the elite of Van Lang society. Eventually, however, official efforts to increase tax revenues irritated the Lac lords and in A.D. 39 sparked a rebellion that led to the temporary eviction of the Han and the restoration of local autonomy. After quelling the revolt, the Han tightened their control over their rebellious subjects and pressed for their forced integration into the Chinese empire.

The Han reconquest of the Red River Delta was a pivotal event in Vietnamese history. No longer a semiautonomous territory at the fringe of the Chinese empire, the area was now exposed to the full force of Sinification. The original Lac state, together with additional territories along the coast to the south, was now directly incorporated into the administrative structure of the Han empire. To undermine the power and influence of the local nobility, a new class of Chinese civilian and military officials was sent south to administer the conquered territory.[3] Undoubtedly, such immigrants brought with them many of the administrative techniques, the cultural preferences, and the social values from the north. For the next several hundred years, Vietnamese society was introduced to Chinese political institutions,

---

between the Chinese and Vietnamese peoples, see Chi Yi-fu, "Chung-kuo min-tsu yu Yueh-nan min-tsu" [The Chinese nationality and the Vietnamese nationality], in Kuo T'ing-yi, ed., *Chung-Yueh wen-hua lun-chi* [Essays on Sino-Vietnamese culture] (Taipei, 1956), pp. 117–132.

[3] For a discussion of the emergence of this new Han-Vietnamese ruling class, see Taylor, pp. 48–54.

Chinese art, architecture, and literature, and even to the Chinese written language.

Despite such assimilative efforts, however, Vietnamese cultural uniqueness and the memory of Vietnamese independence survived. Unlike the other Yueh peoples to the north, who accepted Chinese rule while retaining some elements of their original pre-Han culture, the Vietnamese did not entirely renounce the memory of ancient Van Lang. Much of the pre-Han Lac culture survived under the superficial veneer of Sinification; and although Chinese authority was maintained, periodic revolts demonstrated the stubborn refusal of many Vietnamese to accept the alleged benefits of Chinese rule. Ironically, this streak of independence may have been encouraged, in part, by the class of officials brought in by the Chinese after the revolt in A.D. 39. Many of these officials were gradually integrated into local society and emerged as a new Han-Vietnamese ruling class that increasingly reflected local concerns and resisted domination from the north.[4] In the tenth century, such persistence was rewarded when Vietnamese rebels took advantage of the weakness of the disintegrating Tong (T'ang) dynasty to overthrow Chinese rule and restore Vietnamese independence.

Paradoxically, however, the restoration of an independent Vietnamese state did not result in an end to the cultural borrowing that had taken place in preceding centuries. To the contrary, the introduction of Chinese cultural influence continued unabated, particularly at the official level, where the rulers of the new Vietnamese state found the institutions and values of state Confucianism useful as a means of providing an administrative and ideological foundation for the new Vietnam. Chinese bureaucratic procedures and principles of statecraft strengthened the power and efficiency of the Vietnamese state. The educational system provided a steady stream of recruits trained in the core values of Confucianism for the imperial bureaucracy. The Confucian civil code provided social norms for the edification of the mass of the population. Symbolically, even the Vietnamese name for their new state—*Dai Viet,* or greater Viet—was adopted from the original Chinese name for the peoples along the southern coast.

---

[4] Ibid., pp. 53–54.

The influence of Chinese culture on Vietnamese society, while undoubtedly substantial, should not be exaggerated. In the first place, Chinese practices were often adapted to local conditions. In conformity with the stratified character of existing Vietnamese society, the Chinese civil service examination system, for example, was at first given only to members of the landed aristocracy. Only later did it apply, as in China, to commoners as well.[5] Chinese influence, moreover, was restricted in the main to the ruling class. While Chinese practices prevailed at court and within the bureaucracy, the mass of the population was little affected. Although all Vietnamese were exposed in varying degrees to Confucian ethics, life at the village level, where the majority of the population lived, was still recognizably Vietnamese. Peasant art, architecture, literature, and music continued to reflect traditional folk themes which, more often than not, were indigenous to the local environment, and frequently showed closer resemblance to neighboring societies in Southeast Asia such as Angkor and Champa than to the official culture imported from China.

The same ambiguity marked the political relationship between the two countries. Vietnamese rulers frequently found it prudent to accept the pretensions of superiority and tutelage that China traditionally adopted toward its smaller neighbors. Normally, this was sufficient to deter the Chinese from attempting to reassert their past political domination. Moreover, the tributary relationship was, in various ways, beneficial to the Vietnamese themselves.[6] But acceptance of the tributary relationship did not deter the growth of a strong sense of national consciousness.

---

[5] A similar example can be found in the Confucian civil code which, applied in Vietnam, made a number of gestures to local tradition, including a greater recognition of the rights of women than was the case in China. For a detailed analysis of the Chinese impact on nineteenth-century Vietnam, see Alexander B. Woodside, *Vietnam and the Chinese Model* (Cambridge: Harvard University Press, 1971).

[6] The standard treatment of the tributary system is John K. Fairbank, ed., *The Chinese World Order* (Cambridge: Harvard University Press, 1968). Also see G. Deveria, *Histoire des Relations de la Chine avec l'Annam—Vietnam du XVIe au XIXe Siecle* (Paris: Ernest Leroux, 1980). The tributary state benefited not only from the element of legitimacy that the relationship provided to the local ruling house, but also from access to the vast Chinese market. There are interesting parallels with the relationship between small states and their Great Power sponsors today.

Fiercely jealous of their independence, the Vietnamese reacted quickly whenever their powerful neighbor resumed the effort to restore its political sovereignty. The most prominent example took place in the early fifteenth century, when the Ming dynasty took advantage of civil disorder in Vietnam to restore Chinese rule. Twenty years later, a rebel movement under Le Loi drove the Chinese out and restored Vietnamese independence. Yet the new dynasty continued to make use of Confucian doctrine, and under Le Thanh Tong (1460–1497), one of the greatest of Vietnamese monarchs, it was enshrined as the guiding ideology of the state.

The historical relationship between China and Vietnam, then, was highly idiosyncratic and, in its blend of cultural mimicry and political tension, certainly unique in Southeast Asia. In some respects, it is easier to understand in terms of the complex fraternal relationship between an elder and a younger brother than of the relatively nonhierarchical state-to-state relationship practiced in Western society. To China, the Vietnamese must have resembled a wayward younger brother who stubbornly refused to follow the proper patterns of behavior laid down by the sages of the past. Chinese attitudes toward Vietnam combined paternalism and benevolence with a healthy dose of arrogance and cultural condescension stemming from the conviction that it was China that had lifted the Vietnamese from their previous state of barbarism.[7] As for the Vietnamese, their attitude toward China was a unique blend of respect and truculence, combining a pragmatic acceptance of Chinese power and influence with a dogged defense of Vietnamese independence and distinctiveness. No one symbolized that ambivalence better than Nguyen Trai, the scholar-patriot and military genius who had helped the rebel Le Loi defeat Chinese forces in the early fifteenth century. Nguyen Trai, in a long career dedicated to the service of king and country, combined Confucian orthodoxy in his personal behavior with a fierce sense of Vietnamese patriotism. It is no surprise that he has become the patron saint of the current

---

[7] For an interesting discussion of such attitudes and their origins, see Hisayuki Miyakawa, "The Confucianization of South China," in Arthur F. Wright, ed., *The Confucian Persuasion* (Stanford: Stanford University Press, 1960). Beijing today concedes that China often mistreated Vietnam in the past, but adds that Vietnamese rulers sometimes launched attacks on South China as well. See *Beijing Review,* October 12, 1981, p. 16.

regime in Hanoi, which compares the "patriotic Confucianism" of Nguyen Trai with the puerile sycophancy and servility of the puppet Nguyen court under French rule.[8]

---

[8] For a discussion of the two types of Confucianism in Vietnam, see Chuong Thau, "Nguon goc chu nghia yeu nuoc cua Phan Boi Chau" [The origins of Phan Boi Chau's patriotism], *Nghien Cuu Lich Su* [Historical research, hereafter *NCLS*], no. 88 (July 1966), and Tran Huy Lieu, "Chu nghia anh hung cach mang nuoc ta" [Revolutionary patriotism in our country], *NCLS,* no. 100 (July 1967). Nguyen Trai was the subject of considerable attention among Vietnamese historians in the pages of *NCLS* during the 1960s.

II

China and the Vietnamese Struggle for Independence

The advent of the colonial era transformed the Sino-Vietnamese relationship into a new and unfamiliar shape. When, in the 1880s, the French established a protectorate over North and Central Vietnam (Vietnam's southern provinces had been seized by the French and transformed into the colony of Cochin China two decades earlier), the Qing (Ch'ing) court was forced by treaty to renounce Chinese suzerainty over Vietnam. But although the French conquest brought the tributary relationship to an end, it did not thereby sever the cultural and intellectual bonds that had long existed between the two societies. Western imperialism created a sense of mutual affinity as a result of the shared humiliation that both countries had suffered at the hands of the West. It also created a common challenge and a new cause for collaboration against the mutual enemy. While the Vietnamese could no longer call on the assistance of the Qing dynasty, which was now beginning its own death throes, patriotic intellectuals in Vietnam could turn to their counterparts in China for advice on how to solve the plight facing both countries.

By the end of the nineteenth century the process was well underway. Accustomed to seeking established truth in China, Confucian-trained Vietnamese patriots such as Phan Boi Chau and Phan Chu Trinh sought intellectual guidance from prominent Chinese reformist writers such as Kang Youwei (K'ang Yu-wei) and Liang Qichao (Ling Ch'i-ch'ao). Kang and Liang provided a useful source of ideas about the modern West and how Western values and institutions could be applied to Confucian societies in Asia.[1] Like Kang and Liang, most Vietnamese

---

[1] Liang Qichao's influence on Phan Boi Chau is well known. For a discussion,

patriots of the turn of the century were a product of the Confucian educational system and possessed strong intellectual and emotional ties to the traditional heritage. The writings of the Chinese reformists gave Vietnamese intellectuals reassurance that Western culture could be fruitfully blended with the ancient culture of the East.²

The writings of the Chinese reformists were particularly useful to those Vietnamese intellectuals who were primarily concerned with the long-term cultural impact of the West. They had less appeal to those militants who felt that the immediate priority for patriotic Vietnamese was the eviction of the French. In 1912 Phan Boi Chau, seeking answers, turned again to China, where the revolutionary forces of Sun Yat-sen had just achieved the overthrow of the effete Qing dynasty. To ingratiate himself with Sun, he remodelled his own revolutionary party after Sun's own organization, the Guomindang (Kuomintang). Sun Yat-sen was sympathetic to Chau's request for assistance but preoccupied with his own efforts to consolidate his victory over the old dynasty, and his support for the cause of Vietnamese independence was meager.³

During the next several years the Vietnamese anticolonial movement languished. During the 1920s it began once again to gather momentum with the emergence of a number of political parties and factions formed to seek independence or to pressure the French into granting meaningful reforms. The new genera-

---

see David G. Marr, *Vietnamese Anticolonialism 1885–1925* (Berkeley and Los Angeles: University of California Press, 1971), pp. 109–110, and William J. Duiker, *The Rise of Nationalism in Vietnam, 1900–1941* (Ithaca, N.Y.: Cornell University Press, 1976), pp. 40–41 and 45–48. Kang Youwei's influence on Vietnamese intellectuals is analyzed in Alexander B. Woodside, *Community and Revolution in Vietnam* (Boston: Houghton Mifflin, 1976), pp. 45–53.

² Phan Chu Trinh's attempt to synthesize Confucian ethics with Western values was expressed in two speeches he made in Saigon shortly before his death in 1926. See his "Dao duc va luan ly Dong tay" [Morality and ethics of East and West] and "Quan tri chu nghia va dan tri chu nghia" [Monarchy and democracy] in the September and October 1964 issues of NCLS. Chau's commitment to Confucian ethics is displayed in his *Khong Hoc Dang* [The light of Confucius] (Huê: Anh Minh, 1957).

³ According to Phan Boi Chau's memoirs, Sun promised to provide educational facilities and training to Vietnamese patriots, but no direct support for at least ten years. See *Phan Boi Chau nien bieu* [A chronological biography of Phan Boi Chau] (Hanoi, 1957), p. 144.

tion of Vietnamese nationalists differed in significant respects from their predecessors. Educated in the new school system established by the French, many radical youths of the 1920s had few intellectual or emotional commitments to the Confucian tradition, which they identified with the collaborationist court at Huê, and sought to dethrone "Confucius and sons" and achieve a total "transvaluation of values" by seeking the total Westernization of Vietnamese society.

One consequence of this trend was a decline in Vietnamese intellectual and cultural reliance on China. While some Vietnamese radicals were undoubtedly influenced in their views by the May Fourth movement of the previous decade in China (which itself had been strongly influenced by the West) or by Sun Yat-sen's movement in China (in 1927, for example, a group of young radicals in North Vietnam formed a nationalist party, the *Viet Nam Quoc Dan Dang,* or VNQDD, modeled directly after the Guomindang), in general militant nationalists no longer saw China as a model, but sought the source of national salvation directly from the West.

Not all Vietnamese felt that hasty Westernization was the answer to the problem. Some were convinced that "modernization," to be effective, could not be built in a cultural vacuum but must incorporate elements of the national heritage (*quoc tuy,* or in Chinese *guo cui*). Intellectuals like Phan Khoi and the historian Tran Trong Kim found the answer in a revived Confucianism.[4] The movement was inspired, in part, by similar trends in China, where cultural conservatives attempted to blend Confucian ethics with Western technology. As a number of scholars have pointed out, the effort was somewhat artificial in China (traditionalist, in the words of one scholar, rather than truly "traditional"), but it represented nonetheless a force of considerable emotive power, and a refurbished Confucianism in modern dress eventually became the ideological foundation of the Nanking regime established in 1928 by Sun Yat-sen's successor, Chiang Kai-shek.[5]

---

[4] The best source for information on the intellectual turbulence in post–World War I Vietnam is David G. Marr's monumental *Vietnamese Tradition on Trial* (Berkeley and Los Angeles: University of California Press, 1981). For information on the abortive movement to revive Vietnamese Confucianism, see pp. 105–115. Also see Woodside, *Community and Revolution in Vietnam,* pp. 14–21 and 104–109.

[5] For a discussion, see Joseph Levenson, *Confucian China and Its Modern*

The neo-Confucian movement had less success in Vietnam, and by the 1930s it had petered out. There were probably several reasons for this. First, Confucian ideology lacked the official support in Vietnam that it had received from the Chiang Kai-shek regime in China. While the French paid lip service to traditional morality as a means of curbing political radicalism in schools and villages, they made little effort to utilize it as a source for state ideology. More important as a factor, perhaps, was that Confucianism did not have the deep cultural roots in Vietnam that it did in China, where it was closely identified with the growth of Chinese civilization. Whatever the reasons, most Vietnamese intellectuals seeking native elements to incorporate into their vision for a new society turned not to Confucianism but to indigenous elements from the national tradition. The new trend of cultural nationalism was most visible in literature, and the primary vehicle was *quoc ngu,* a Latin-based script for written Vietnamese first developed by Western missionaries in the seventeenth century. Although the system had been invented as a tool to teach the scriptures and was first rejected by patriots as a Western invention, progressive intellectuals, recognizing its potential value as a national symbol and its practical superiority over the cumbersome if aesthetically beautiful Chinese system of ideographs, soon accepted it, and by the 1920s it was widely in use as a vehicle for promoting the revival of the national literary tradition. Novelists, dramatists, and poets used the script to create a new vernacular literature, based on a mixture of indigenous and Western traditions, and *quoc ngu* began to emerge as a symbol of the rise of a new national consciousness.

The Birth of Vietnamese Communism

In the early 1920s a new form of political and social radicalism began to penetrate Vietnam from the West. Until the outbreak of the Russian revolution in 1917, Marxist ideas had been little known outside the Western world. But the rise to power of the Bolsheviks in Russia appeared to demonstrate the relevance of Marxist ideology to preindustrial societies in Asia, where it soon began to exert a significant impact on radical circles. After the foundation of the Communist International

---

Fate, vol. 3, *The Problem of Intellectual Continuity* (London: Routledge and Kegan Paul, 1958), chaps. 7 and 9.

(Comintern) in 1919, Comintern agents fanned out to the East to promote the cause of social revolution there. The new doctrine made immediate inroads in China, and in the summer of 1921 a Chinese Communist Party (CCP) was founded in Shanghai. Four years later the Vietnamese radical patriot Ho Chi Minh (then known as Nguyen Ai Quoc) founded the first Marxist organization in French Indochina, the Vietnamese Revolutionary Youth League.

From the outset, the destinies of the two parties appeared to be inseparably linked. Both were the direct product of a rising wave of antiimperialism sweeping through Asia. Both found their immediate appeal among radical intellectuals who sought to create a global alliance of the downtrodden masses against Western colonial authority and the lingering power of Asian feudal reaction. Because the CCP was founded a few years earlier than the league and was able to operate in the relatively safe confines of Gwangdong (Kwangtung) province (where its ally, Sun's Guomindang, had a revolutionary base), Comintern headquarters in Moscow assigned it leadership responsibilities for other revolutionary parties in colonial Southeast Asia. The CCP was particularly useful to the league, which, to avoid the repressive efforts of the French *Sureté,* established its own headquarters in Canton (now commonly known as Guangzhou), the capital of Gwangdong province. New members of the league were routinely sent to Canton for political and ideological training at a Vietnamese training school connected with Sun's Whampoa Academy. Several members of the league joined the CCP.[6]

Such ties were somewhat misleading, however, for the league's most direct and intimate relationship was not with the CCP but with the Comintern in Moscow. It was the Comintern that had provided Ho Chi Minh with the training and the guidance to form a Marxist revolutionary party in Vietnam. It was the Comintern that provided most of the financial support for the league as well as its strategical direction. And it was to the Comintern's Stalin School in Moscow that, beginning in 1927, the most promising young league members were sent for ideolog-

---

[6] For information on the league's operations in South China, see my *The Comintern and Vietnamese Communism* (Athens: Ohio University Press, 1975), and Huynh Kim Khanh, *Vietnamese Communism, 1925–1945* (Ithaca, N.Y.: Cornell University Press, 1982).

ical and organizational training as the nucleus of a future Vietnamese Communist Party.[7]

The league's primary link with Moscow was strengthened by the course of events in Asia. When Chiang Kai-shek cracked down on CCP activities in Canton in April 1927, Ho Chi Minh was forced to flee, and the league established a new headquarters in the British crown colony of Hong Kong. For a few years the league was able to maintain its relationship with the CCP through the Comintern's Far Eastern Bureau in Shanghai, but these tenuous ties were broken entirely when Chiang Kai-shek cracked down on Communist operations there in 1931. The Far Eastern Bureau collapsed when the CCP was forced to establish a new base of operations in the mountains of Jiangxi (Kiangsi) province, where Mao Zedong had established a guerrilla base after the breakup of the Communist-Guomindang alliance in 1927. In 1934 even that base had to be abandoned, and the party set up its new headquarters in Yan'an (Yenan), far to the north.[8]

Its links with the CCP now almost nonexistent, the league (which had transformed itself into a formal Indochinese Communist Party, or ICP, in 1930) was now forced to orient its attention even more firmly in the direction of Moscow. After an abortive rebellion in Central Vietnam in the fall of 1930 virtually destroyed the party, the original leaders, many of whom were either dead or in prison, were replaced by graduates of the Stalin School whose ideological views were strongly influenced by the Soviet Union. The results were not uniformly beneficial. In its early years the league had earned considerable appeal in Vietnam through its emphasis on national independence and a populist approach directed at earning the support of the peasants, intellectuals, and urban workers alike. After 1928, however, the Comintern shifted its ideological course and began to stress the impor-

---

[7] The most complete source of information about the Stalin School and its training program for young Vietnamese is the colonial archives in Paris. The French had relatively good access to the operations of the school through information provided by double agents.

[8] As an indication of the effect of such events on links between the two revolutionary organizations, Ho Chi Minh once noted that on his release from a Hong Kong prison in 1933 he was only able to arrange contact with the CCP through a letter dropped at the Shanghai home of Sun Yat-sen's widow, Soong Qingling (Soong Ch'ing-ling), who was sympathetic to the party's revolutionary goals.

tance of class struggle and the leading role of the proletariat in building a communist movement. The new leadership of the ICP was in the grip of this narrow sectarian mentality, and during the early 1930s party propaganda downgraded patriotic themes and the role of the peasant in the revolutionary process. Was Ho Chi Minh, now in the Soviet Union allegedly recovering from an illness, in Stalin's disfavor, as some suspect? Can the Vietnamese Stalin School graduates be compared with the "28 Bolsheviks," who attempted unsuccessfully to implant Stalin's views on the CCP? Unfortunately, little is known about this period in the history of the ICP or its leading members. Perhaps the answer can be found in the Comintern archives.[9]

This phase in the history of the Vietnamese revolutionary movement came to an end with the approach of World War II. The rise of Adolf Hitler in Germany compelled Moscow to reassess its overall global strategy from one emphasizing class struggle toward one of seeking a popular front with Western democracies against the common threat of world fascism. In Indochina the impact of this reorientation served to permit the ICP to emerge from the wilderness whence it had been banished by Comintern strategy and to compete in the political arena for the support of the various classes and political forces in French Indochina. The ICP's freedom was enhanced after the Soviet entrance into the European War in 1941. Preoccupied with its own problems, Moscow now permitted Asian communist parties greater latitude in the determination of their own policies.

Meanwhile, the approach of war in Asia also brought the ICP back in direct contact, for the first time since the early 1930s, with the communist movement in China. The primary instrument of contact was Ho Chi Minh himself. In 1938, after

---

[9] Historians in Vietnam today deny any split between "nationalist" and "internationalist" elements in the ICP during this period. According to Van Tao, director of the Institute of History in Hanoi, although individual party members may have leaned toward one or another approach, in general the global perspectives of ICP leaders mirrored those at Comintern headquarters in Moscow and shifted toward a more nationalist approach, along with Soviet policy, in the late 1930s. I am inclined to believe that divergent views may have existed but not to the point of provoking a serious split in the party, which was reduced to a sheer struggle for survival in the early 1930s. As for Ho Chi Minh himself, he may have disagreed with the class line of the Comintern but for the moment kept his own counsel. For a discussion, see Khanh, *Vietnamese Communism,* pp. 173–178, and Duiker, *The Comintern,* pp. 24–27.

five years in the Soviet Union, he returned to China, where he reportedly spent a few weeks at Communist headquarters in Yan'an and then traveled to South China, where he served in various capacities with CCP units stationed in the area. It is unfortunate that so little information is available on his activities in China and the impact they might have had on his own ideas. There is no doubt that the Maoist strategy of people's war bore a distinct resemblance to the strategy that emerged, under Ho Chi Minh's prodding, after the famous ICP Eighth Plenum in 1941. Moreover, after his return to head the ICP, Ho Chi Minh arranged for the translation into Vietnamese of a number of Chinese manuals on guerrilla warfare for the use of the party's military forces. On the other hand, much of the new revolutionary strategy, as scholars in Vietnam today point out, was the product of ideas that Ho Chi Minh had in mind since the 1920s. Perhaps the most dispassionate judgment that can be made without further evidence is that Ho found the Maoist model congenial in some respects to his own ideas and borrowed those elements that he considered appropriate for application in Vietnam.[10]

Whatever the truth, the culmination of these trends arrived with the formation in the spring of 1941 of the famous *Viet Nam Doc Lap Dong Minh* (League for the Independence of Vietnam), better known as the Vietminh Front. At a plenary session of the Central Committee chaired by Ho Chi Minh, the party formally approved the adoption of a new strategy that emphasized the issues of national independence and land reform. At the same time, a new military strategy based on the buildup of guerrilla units to fight against French colonial rule and Japanese occupation forces in revolutionary base areas in the mountains of North

---

[10] Historians in Hanoi today are understandably at pains to dissociate the famous "Vietminh" strategy from any taint of the legacy of Maoism. For example, see Van Tao, "Nhung net khac nhau giua cach mang Viet Nam va cach mang Trung quoc" [The differences between the Vietnamese and the Chinese revolutions], NCLS, no. 190 (January-February 1980). For an analysis of Ho Chi Minh's influence on Vietnamese revolutionary strategy, see my *The Communist Road to Power in Vietnam* (Boulder, Colo.: Westview Press, 1981), passim, esp. pp. 64–72. For a brief discussion of Ho's activities in China, see King C. Chen, *Vietnam and China, 1938–1954* (Princeton, N.J.: Princeton University Press, 1969), pp. 34–37. One source claims that Ho joined the CCP during this period. See Chiang Yung-ching, *Hu Chih-ming tsai Chung-kuo* [Ho Chi Minh in China] (Taipei: Chuan-chi Wen-hsueh, 1972), p. 94.

Vietnam was adopted. The headquarters of the party, however, would be established for the time being in South China, where it would be safe from attack by French or Japanese forces.

The decision to use the border area with China as a sanctuary restored the physical importance of China to the fortunes of the Vietnamese revolution. The Vietminh also sought active military and political assistance from Chinese Nationalist authorities in the southern provinces for their own anti-Japanese activities in Vietnam. Official aid from China was limited because Chinese authorities were suspicious of the communist complexion of the Vietminh Front. Ho Chi Minh's efforts to cultivate amicable relations with Chinese authorities did not go entirely unrewarded, however, for as a result of the tolerant attitude of Zhang Faguei (Chang Fa-kuei), the Nationalist military commander in the area, the Vietminh were able to operate in South China with little interference from local authorities.

A final consequence of the Pacific War on the fortunes of the Vietnamese communist movement was its undermining effect on French authority in Indochina. Reduced to titular status in 1940 by Japanese military occupation, the French colonial administration was formally abolished by the Japanese in March 1945. Japan's surrender in August created in Vietnam a political vacuum that the party quickly and effectively filled. Seizing control of much of Vietnam during the so-called August Revolution, the Vietminh declared the creation of a provisional republican government with Ho Chi Minh as president. During the next several months the new government, now formally named the Democratic Republic of Vietnam (DRV), was able to consolidate its authority in North and Central Vietnam while the area was still under occupation by Chinese expeditionary forces. The South remained under French control. The following March, by treaty with France, Chinese troops were withdrawn and a small contingent of French troops was introduced into the DRV. In a separate "preliminary" agreement, Ho and French representative Jean Sainteny agreed on a settlement calling for the formation of a Vietnamese "free state" within the French Union. Ho justified the decision to his colleagues by observing that it was better for his countrymen to sniff French excrement for a brief period than to eat Chinese excrement for the rest of their lives.[11]

---

[11] Space does not permit a detailed account of Ho's strategy during this

Ho's gamble that the French could be persuaded to abandon their colony in Indochina voluntarily did not succeed. By fall the fragile agreement negotiated in March had virtually collapsed, and in December war erupted. During the next several years, faced with the realization that the struggle against the French would require a substantial military effort and that aid from their major sponsor, the USSR, would be minimal, party leaders turned once again to China.[12]

Prospects for aid from the CCP in the prosecution of the struggle against the French were not immediately promising, since Mao's forces were themselves involved in a growing civil conflict with the government of Chiang Kai-shek. But the Vietnamese did draw on Chinese experience to formulate a strategy to defeat the militarily stronger French forces in Indochina. In 1947, as the conflict began, the DRV formally proclaimed that it would adopt the Maoist strategy of people's war, calling for a three-stage conflict moving from withdrawal and avoidance of conflict through guerrilla struggle and culminating in a strategic general offensive to drive the enemy's forces out of the major cities.[13] In the fall of 1949 prospects for victory improved dramatically with the final victory of communist forces in China and the promulgation of the People's Republic of China (PRC). The new regime in Beijing represented a potentially decisive trump card for the Vietnamese revolutionary movement, and the party moved quickly to take advantage of the opportunity. In

---

period, which in any case is not essential to our analysis. For a useful discussion, see King C. Chen, chap. 3.

[12] The Soviet Union showed little interest in the conflict in Indochina in the years following World War II. Moscow was preoccupied with the situation in Europe, and Stalin apparently gave little attention to the prospects for revolution in Asia. According to reliable sources, the Soviet Union actually instructed the ICP to moderate its activities in Indochina to avoid embarrassing the French Communist Party, which briefly shared power in a coalition government after World War II. The standard account of Soviet foreign policy in Southeast Asia is Charles B. McLane, *Soviet Strategies in Southeast Asia* (Princeton, N.J.: Princeton University Press, 1966). See especially pp. 261–278.

[13] The best known source on Vietnamese strategy during this period is Truong Chinh's *The Resistance Will Win*, which drew liberally on Mao's *On Protracted War*, written in 1938. Truong Chinh's essay (in English) is in Truong Chihn, *Primer for Revolt* (New York: Praeger, 1963). Mao's article "On Protracted War" can be found in *Selected Writings of Mao Tse-tung* (Peking: Foreign Languages Press, 1972). For an analysis and references, see my *The Communist Road*, pp. 138–141.

January 1950 Ho Chi Minh went secretly to China to seek a military aid agreement that would provide assistance to Vietminh forces in the war against the French.

In Beijing, Ho found a receptive audience. While the primary objective of the new Chinese leadership was undoubtedly to promote economic construction and the communist consolidation of power on the mainland, Chinese leaders also had several key concerns regarding foreign affairs. Their immediate priority was to secure the fruits of the revolution from a counterattack by the aggressive forces of U.S. imperialism. To that end, China chose to "lean to one side," to establish an alliance with the USSR despite the Chinese conviction that Moscow had provided the CCP with inadequate assistance in its civil war against Chiang Kai-shek.[14] In the longer perspective, however, Chinese national security could be achieved only through the reconstitution in modern guise of the security perimeter of surrounding friendly states which had been the traditional objective of Chinese foreign policy during the imperial era and which had been substantially eaten away during the age of Western imperialism. The southern border with Vietnam was probably not the area of greatest sensitivity along the frontier. Chinese leaders were undoubtedly more concerned over Taiwan (now the home of Chiang Kai-shek's Republic of China), Korea (where U.S. military forces still occupied the southern half of the peninsula), and Manchuria (where the Soviet Union still possessed "pre-eminent interests" and a naval base at Port Arthur). Still, it was through its control over Indochina that France had been able to extend its influence into the southern Chinese provinces during the declining years of the Qing dynasty, and continued imperialist occupation of the area could provide Beijing's immediate major enemy, the United States, with a means of pressuring China from the south. A victory in some form for the revolutionary forces in Vietnam was clearly in the Chinese national interest.

The foreign policy of the new China, of course, was not formulated in an ideological vacuum. To Chinese leaders, the nature of the world, and China's place in it, was reflected through the prism of Marxist doctrine and the historical experience of the Chinese Communist Party. The teachings of Marx and Lenin

---

[14] See John Gittings, *The World and China, 1922-1972* (New York: Harper, 1974), p. 115.

taught that the world was entering a period of intense conflict between the forces of declining capitalism and emerging socialism. Marx and Lenin, understandably Eurocentric in their geographical orientation, saw the critical battles taking place in the West. Mao Zedong and his colleagues had a somewhat different perspective. Viewed from Beijing, the key struggles were likely to take place in the intermediate zone of Asia, Africa, and Latin America, where the oppressed masses were preparing to rise up to overthrow the reactionary forces of global imperialism. The Chinese revolution represented a critical moment in this extended historical process, and now the Maoist concept of people's war could provide a model for struggles of national liberation elsewhere in the Third World. For the immediate future, Chinese spokesmen made clear, the insurgency movements in Malaya and Indochina were the best cases in point.[15]

To China's new leaders, then, the situation in Vietnam represented the convergence of two key factors in the foreign policy of the new regime—the issue of national interest (by means of which China could protect its vital southern flank against imperialist control) and the issue of revolutionary obligation (through which China could fulfill its task of "proletarian internationalism," by assisting a fraternal communist party and promoting the surge of a revolutionary wave to drive imperialism from Asian shores).[16]

In January 1950 China rewarded Ho's visit by becoming the first country to recognize the DRV. Three months later the two states announced the signing of a military aid agreement according to which the PRC would provide the Vietminh with military equipment and the training of personnel for the latter's struggle against the French in Indochina. During the next several months a Chinese military assistance group under General Wei Guoqing (Wei Kuo-ch'ing) was sent, reportedly at Ho Chi Minh's request, to advise the Vietminh on military strategy. A training mission led by Vice Minister of Defense Zheng Geng

---

[15] The most famous exposition of this view was Liu Shaoqi's speech at the World Trade Union conference held in Beijing in November 1949. Liu's speech was reported by the New China News Agency (NCN) on November 23, 1949. For a discussion of the speech and its implications, see Melvin Gurtov, *The First Vietnam Crisis* (New York: Columbia University Press, 1967), pp. 7–8, and King C. Chen, pp. 214–220.

[16] Gurtov, p. 7.

(Cheng Keng) arrived to train cadres and troops, and a training school was set up in South China. Shipments of weapons, ammunition, and other military provisions began to cross the border in increasing quantities.[17]

Some outside observers would later assert that Chinese assistance was the critical factor that enabled the Vietminh to defeat the French. Such a statement probably underplays the role of indigenous factors within Vietnam itself. It is nonetheless true that with Chinese aid the fortunes of the Vietminh began rapidly to improve, and party leaders in Vietnam began to escalate the level of their struggle against the French. In the fall of 1950, Vietminh forces, now armed with weapons from China, launched a major offensive that drove the French out of the border region and opened the area to Vietminh control. French observers reported that the Vietminh were operating with a new aggressiveness and, for the first time, had begun to attack in regimental formations, causing heavy casualties to French units in the area. The following spring party strategists, following the precepts of people's war and probably with the full consultation of Chinese advisers, attempted to shift to the third stage of general offensive, in a series of "human wave" attacks on French military positions on the fringes of the Red River Delta.

Continuing Vietminh interest in the Chinese model was also reflected in the areas of political organization and social and economic policy. In February 1951, at the Second National Congress of the ICP (now renamed the Vietnam Workers' Party, or VWP), party spokesmen referred on several occasions to the value of Chinese experience for the construction of a socialist society in Vietnam and described the DRV, in Maoist terms, as a "people's democratic dictatorship." Later that year a team of Chinese administrative experts under Lo Guibo (Luo Kuei-po) arrived in Vietnam to provide advice on finance, economics, land reform, and the training of cadres (*zheng feng,* known in Vietnamese as *chinh huan*).[18]

---

[17] For sources, see King C. Chen, pp. 260–262; Gurtov, pp. 12–14; and Jay Taylor, *China and Southeast Asia* (New York: Praeger, 1976), pp. 5–6.

[18] For a brief reference to the adoption of Chinese concepts during this period, see Nguyen Khac Vien, "Les specialistes du discours politique creux aux postes clefs et l'inflation bureaucratique," in Georges Boudarel et al., eds., *La bureaucratie au Vietnam* (Paris: l'Harmattan, 1983), p. 119. For an analysis, see King C. Chen, pp. 240–249.

The apparent turn to China in 1950 and 1951 marked an important stage in the history of the Vietnamese revolution, and has provoked debate over the motives and the environment surrounding the decision. Was the decision to adopt the Chinese model voluntary or was it, as has been claimed, a condition for assistance exacted by the PRC? Did China persuade Vietnamese leaders to abandon the relatively moderate and broad-based national front strategy in favor of a more orthodox approach stressing the core values of Marxism-Leninism, or was the shift adopted by the VWP for its own reasons? The lack of reliable sources makes it difficult to reach definitive answers to such questions. Still, tentative answers might be in order. Chinese leaders undoubtedly expected the Vietnamese to follow their advice, and the effusive praise in the DRV press about the value of such experience suggests that the Vietnamese viewed their adoption of the Maoist model, at least in part, as payment for Chinese assistance (one is inescapably reminded of Phan Boi Chau's efforts to obtain support from Sun Yat-sen by similar means forty years earlier). Ho Chi Minh had learned long ago the value of flattering a potential beneficiary. On the other hand, there is no compelling evidence that the Vietnamese resented Chinese advice or felt compelled against their judgment to shift their own approach to conform to the wishes of Beijing. In all likelihood, party leaders viewed Chinese experience as useful and felt that they would benefit from it.[19]

China, Vietnam, and the Conference at Geneva

Was Chinese assistance a major factor in leading the Vietminh to its partial victory at the conference table in 1954? That question aroused a good deal of partisan debate during the long Indochina conflict, and it continues to provoke bitter controversy between China and Vietnam today. Beijing has claimed that Chinese aid was substantial, and crucial to Vietminh success on

---

[19] A similar view is apparently held by historians in Hanoi. In response to a question relating to the period, Professor Van Tao remarked that in his opinion, Vietnamese party leaders at that time considered Chinese revolutionary experience useful and were prepared to make use of it. So far as he knew, Chinese experience was adopted voluntarily and not as the result of pressure from Beijing. For example, the tactic of negotiating and fighting simultaneously came from Chinese experience in the Korean War. Interview with Van Tao at the Institute of History in Hanoi, December 10, 1985.

the battlefield. Before the battle of Dien Bien Phu, China contends, assistance from the PRC increased dramatically, and the battle itself was planned with the aid of Chinese advisers. Hanoi has countered that Chinese aid was "tiny" and not a major factor in Vietminh success. Moreover, assert the Vietnamese, Chinese strategical advice was not always effective. According to one senior staff officer of the People's Army of Vietnam (PAVN): "If we had used Chinese strategy we would have lost the war."[20]

The dispute over the effectiveness of Chinese strategy is of particular interest, since it was widely assumed during the recent war that Hanoi owed a considerable debt to the Maoist concept of people's war. The evidence suggests, however, that Vietnamese planners may have developed serious reservations about the relevance of Chinese strategy to conditions in Vietnam even before the end of the Franco-Vietminh conflict. The first indication may have come as early as 1951, when the attempt to advance to the "third stage" of general offensive resulted in high Vietminh casualties and minimum success on the battlefield. Hanoi has not directly blamed Chinese advice for the disaster, but party strategists did return to a more cautious approach after the Delta offensive, and Vietminh strategists may have begun to question the value of the concept of people's war in Vietnam. These doubts apparently resurfaced at Dien Bien Phu, when Vietnamese military commanders reportedly rejected Chinese advice to adopt "human wave" tactics and adopted a more cautious approach which led to the gradual infestation of French lines and the overrunning of the base on May 6, on the eve of the convening of the discussions on Indochina at Geneva. Hanoi now openly charges that Chinese concepts were not suitable to conditions in Vietnam.

The question of the inadequacy of Chinese military assistance is somewhat more difficult to answer. According to estimates provided by U.S. sources, the level of Chinese military aid increased significantly from an average of ten to twenty tons a month in 1951 to several hundred tons a month two years later.

---

[20] The Vietnamese officer was Hoang Van Thai, now a deputy Minister of Defense. See his article in *Tap Chi Cong San* (March 1984), translated in JPRS 84,084. for a corroborating analysis, see Georges Boudarel, "Comment Giap a failli perdre la bataille de Dien Bien Phu," *Le Nouvel Observateur,* April 8, 1983. China's claims are contained in *Beijing Review,* November 23 and 30, 1979, and October 12, 1981.

Unquestionably, this assistance was a major factor in the Vietminh victory at Dien Bien Phu. Hanoi, however, charges that, far from desiring a Vietminh victory, Beijing feared the emergence of a strong and unified Vietnam. Chinese strategy was thus designed to keep Indochina divided in order to facilitate Chinese domination of the area in the future. That charge is based on several contentions: (1) that China refused to provide maximum assistance to the Vietminh in late 1953 and 1954 in order to compel the DRV to accept a negotiated settlement, (2) that at the Geneva Conference in the spring and summer of 1954 the Chinese negotiators persuaded the Vietnamese delegation to accept a division of Vietnam, which would be disadvantageous to the struggle for national reunification, and (3) that China's chief negotiator, Zhou Enlai, conspired with the Western powers to reject representation by the delegations of the revolutionary movements in Laos and Cambodia, thus thwarting the legitimate rights of the revolutionary movements in the two countries.[21]

The first charge, that Beijing attempted to use its assistance as a lever to persuade the Vietnamese to accept a negotiated settlement of the Indochina conflict, may have some basis in fact. By late 1953 the "revolutionary" phase that had characterized Chinese foreign policy since 1949 had come to an end. Chinese participation in the Korean War had been costly, in terms of casualties as well as in its impact on domestic reconstruction. Moreover, it had illustrated the dangers that could result from an active involvement by China in the emerging Cold War struggle. The United States had not behaved like a "paper tiger," as Mao had earlier predicted, but had indicated a disconcerting willingness to intervene in Asia. For its part, the Soviet Union, while helping to provoke the Korean conflict, had allowed China to bear the brunt of its human and material costs. The end result had been ambivalent, at best. Beijing's participation in the conflict had prevented the unification of the peninsula under the anticommunist government in the South. But Chinese intervention had aroused the hostility of the United States, which now viewed the Beijing regime as a malignant force in Asia, and con-

---

[21] The most authoritative source for Hanoi's views on the Chinese role at Geneva is the Vietnamese white paper, *The Truth about Vietnamo-Chinese Relations over the Past Thirty Years,* issued by the SRV Ministry of Foreign Affairs in 1979.

sequently had offered its protection to the Chiang Kai-shek regime.

The events in Korea undoubtedly had an impact on the overall foreign policy perceptions in Beijing. Whether or not Chinese leaders had desired a total victory in Indochina for Vietminh forces in 1950, they presumably had no desire to see China directly involved in the conflict. This became even more true after the outbreak of war in Korea and the growing level of U.S. involvement in the Franco-Vietminh conflict. An escalation of the level of fighting in Indochina could unleash uncontrollable forces that could bring Beijing and Washington into direct confrontation, a course of events that Chinese leaders ardently desired to prevent. By 1951, then, China's desire to fulfill its fraternal obligations in Vietnam was constrained by an even stronger determination to avoid provoking greater U.S. involvement in the conflict, and several observers have noted that Chinese aid to the Vietminh was carefully calibrated to keep the situation from getting out of hand.[22]

By late 1953 such considerations had assumed an even greater importance. It now became clear to Chinese leaders that a further escalation of the crisis could lead to direct confrontation with the United States. In September, U.S. Secretary of State John Foster Dulles had threatened direct U.S. retaliation against the Chinese mainland should PRC aid to Vietnam increase. In October, as negotiations brought the Korean conflict to an end, Chinese sources began to hint at the possibility of a negotiated settlement of the conflict in Indochina.[23]

Against such conclusions, of course, is the fact that Chinese assistance to the Vietminh increased dramatically in late 1953 and early 1954. Yet here, too, the evidence suggests that such aid was designed, above all, at promoting a political settlement of the war favorable to China. At the outset of the conflict, when the DRV was isolated internationally and Vietminh forces were much weaker than those of the French, Ho Chi Minh sought a compromise solution with the French, who rejected his initiatives. By the early 1950s, however, the momentum of the conflict had changed radically. With Chinese aid on the increase,

---

[22] François Joyaux, *La Chine et le Règlement du Premier Conflit d'Indochine*, (Genève, 1954), (Paris: Sorbonne, 1979), p. 71, and Gurtov, p. 14.

[23] Joyaux, p. 68; Jay Taylor, p. 11.

and support for the war effort declining in France, optimism within the Vietminh camp must have been on the rise, and it is likely that party leaders sensed the possibility of achieving a total military victory throughout Indochina.[24]

The Vietminh, however, could not hope for such a victory with a continued high level of support from the PRC. This, of course, increased the risk of direct U.S. involvement, and a widening conflict over Indochina. Such considerations, however, were understandably of lower priority to party leaders in Vietnam than they were to the Chinese, and the Vietnamese may well have been skeptical of Beijing's claims that greater Vietminh successes on the battlefield could increase the risk of a wider war.

The Vietnamese, then, may have sensed a sell-out by their major socialist allies since Moscow, for its own reasons, had also indicated an interest in a negotiated settlement. In this environment, DRV leaders may have agreed to attend peace talks only on condition that China agree to provide a higher level of military assistance to enable the Vietminh to achieve a more favorable situation on the battlefield. The battle of Dien Bien Phu was the direct result of that bargain, and there is no doubt that the fall of that military base on May 6, the eve of the convening of the talks, substantially improved the DRV's bargaining position at the conference table. On November 20, three weeks after French prime Minister Joseph Laniel had indicated an interest in the conference, Ho Chi Minh informed a Swedish journalist of Vietnamese willingness to attend a conference to seek peace in Indochina. A few days later the PRC indicated its approval in an article in *People's Daily*.[25]

Hanoi's doubts about the constancy of Chinese support resurfaced at the conference. According to Vietnamese sources,

---

[24] Against this conclusion must be set the comment by Nikita Khrushchev that Ho Chi Minh had told Zhou Enlai in 1954 that the military situation was "hopeless" and that the Vietnamese desperately needed a cease-fire. Khrushchev's views are suspect, of course, since his relations with Vietnamese leaders were notoriously poor. See *Khrushchev Remembers* (New York: Bantam, 1971), p. 533.

[25] Joyaux, p. 91; Gurtov, p. 18. According to the Vietnamese defector Hoang Van Hoan, the VWP leadership agreed to participate in negotiations after long discussion. See his interview published in the *Beijing Review,* December 7, 1979, p. 13. For the Vietnamese decision to attack Dien Bien Phu, and its role in the party's revolutionary strategy, see Boudarel, "Comment Giap," and my *The Communist Road,* pp. 158–162.

China's chief delegate Zhou Enlai, in an effort to promote a compromise, forced DRV negotiators to accept a regroupment zone for the Vietminh forces smaller than the one the latter had demanded at the conference. Zhou also supported the Western demand to schedule reunification elections two years after the close of the conference, rather than the shorter period proposed by the DRV. The longer period demanded by the Western representatives would provide the noncommunist forces greater opportunity to organize a government in the South.[26] Finally, Hanoi contends that Zhou conspired with Western delegations to prevent representatives of the insurgency movements in Laos and Cambodia from attending the conference alongside delegates from the royal governments of those two countries.

Such charges are angrily rejected by the PRC, which has claimed that all decisions between the communist delegations at the conference were reached unanimously and that Ho Chi Minh had fully recognized the need to seek a settlement to prevent U.S. entry into the conflict. The latter point is not implausible. Ho had always carefully nurtured good relations with his socialist allies, and he undoubtedly recognized the need to cater to their concerns at Geneva. Moreover, Ho Chi Minh, the only Vietnamese leader with substantial international experience, was undoubtedly more aware of the danger of U.S. entry into the war. Ho may well have been forced to use his considerable powers of persuasion to bring his militant colleagues to accept the concessions necessary to bring about a settlement.[27]

Still, there appears to be some validity to Hanoi's charge that Beijing, for its own reasons, pressured the DRV into making a number of substantial concessions at the conference. Available evidence suggests not only that Zhou Enlai was instrumental in

---

[26] *The Truth*, pp. 23–26.

[27] Ho had played such a role on at least two previous occasions, when he persuaded firebrands in the ICP to accept the Ho-Sainteny agreement in March 1946 and in the fall of the same year, when ne negotiated a modus vivendi with the French government to delay the outbreak of war. For China's response, see "On Hanoi's White Book," *Beijing Review*, November 23, 1979. Beijing's contention is supported by Hoang Van Hoan, who stated after his arrival in Beijing in 1979 that the decision to accept the seventeenth parallel had been made with the full concurrence of the DRV leadership. Nikita Khrushchev appears to agree. According to his memoirs, the socialist delegations "gasped with surprise and pleasure" when the French accepted the dividing line at the seventeenth parallel. See *Khrushchev Remembers*, p. 534.

overcoming the differences between the two sides over key issues, but that on at least some of the occasions mentioned above he apparently sided with the Western rather than the Vietnamese point of view and forced the latter into meaningful concessions. If such is the case, it is no wonder the Vietnamese felt betrayed.

The fact is, China's objectives at the conference, and its perspective on future trends in Asia, differed in substantial respects from those of the DRV. Where most DRV leaders viewed the needs of the Vietnamese revolution as the issue of highest priority and feared a compromise settlement that might place serious roadblocks on the road to national reunification, China could see a number of advantages in a compromise agreement. A negotiated settlement, for instance, would reduce the growing threat of direct confrontation with the United States and permit China to turn its attention to pressing issues of economic development.[28] It would lead to a reduction in tension in Southeast Asia, involving the removal of Western military forces from Indochina and the creation of a ring of neutral but friendly states along China's southern perimeter. Finally, a settlement might even set the stage for an improvement in China's relations with the West and bring to an end Chinese isolation from world affairs. By playing a constructive role in the peacemaking process at Geneva, Beijing could enhance its status and hasten its acceptance as a legitimate member of the international community.

There was, of course, an ideological price to pay, for China's new policy of moderation left it open to the charge of betraying the interests of the world revolution—a charge that Hanoi today has been quick to make. Yet China's leaders must have justified their actions by pointing out that revolution cannot be forced, but rises and falls in cycles, and that a strong China could play a more effective role when the next revolutionary wave began to surge. If necessary, of course, they could cite classical precedent—Lenin's decision to settle with Germany at Brest-Litovsk in 1918, or Stalin's decision in the mid-1930s to promote Popular Fronts with the Western democracies against

---

[28] The cardinal importance of domestic issues as an element in the making of Chinese foreign policy has been noted by a number of China watchers. For a recent interpretation, see Melvin Gurtov and Byong-moo Hwang, *China Under Threat* (Baltimore, Md.: The Johns Hopkins University Press, 1980).

the common threat of world fascism. The theory and practice of Marxism-Leninism, like that of most ideologies, is sufficiently ambiguous to permit flexible interpretations of holy writ.

To what degree Vietnamese party leaders accepted the logic behind Chinese actions at the conference is difficult to say with certainty. At a minimum they may have taken issue with Beijing's (and Moscow's) view that the needs of world communism took precedence over those of the Vietnamese revolution. In any event, the Vietnamese had a more ominous interpretation for China's behavior. To the Vietnamese, China's actions at Geneva were not motivated solely by the desire to seek a peaceful resolution of the Indochina conflict, but had a more primordial character, to maintain the weakness and division of Indochina and thus to facilitate Chinese domination over the area in the future. While one aspect of that strategy could have been seen in Zhou Enlai's support for a divided Vietnam, the most visible manifestation could be found in Beijing's policy toward Laos and Cambodia.

To understand the apparent conflict of interest between China and the DRV over Laos and Cambodia, it is necessary to take a brief foray into history. During the precolonial period China had successfully maintained tributary relations with both states but had never exercised direct political control over either, and the cultural institutions of the two countries were influenced more by the Indian than by the Sinic tradition. Vietnamese involvement had been more frequent and more direct. Throughout the traditional period the Vietnamese empire was in frequent contact with both states, and in the nineteenth century, at a time when both Laos and Cambodia were in a period of decline, Vietnam was able to exercise a degree of informal suzerainty over both countries. This process might have resulted in the eventual absorption of the two into the Vietnamese empire had not the process been interrupted by the French conquest and the creation of separate protectorates.

In its infancy the ICP had expressed little interest in either country. Concerned primarily with the issue of national independence and convinced that Laos and Cambodia were not only different in culture but also more primitive in their economic and social development, Vietnamese Marxists at first saw little relevance for these areas to the Vietnamese revolution. The first formal linkage took place in October 1930 when the new Vietnamese Communist Party, which had been established by Ho Chi Minh in February, was renamed the Indochinese Communist Party (*Dang Cong San Dong Duong*) at the instruction of the Comintern in Moscow.[29]

Until World War II the ICP took little note of the "Indochinese" character of the movement, and the handful of party cells that were formed in the two protectorates consisted mainly of ethnic Vietnamese living in the two countries. Party documents talked vaguely of an "Indochinese Federation" to be formed after the victory of the three peoples over French imperialism, but many Vietnamese party members had serious doubts that the protectorates of Laos and Cambodia were ripe for revolution, and the concept of a close federation began to assume importance in the minds of ICP leaders only in the late 1940s, when Vietminh strategists began to realize the importance of creating an Indochina-wide theater of operations in order to force the French to disperse their forces and create opportunities for local military operations. Radical movements had just begun to emerge in both countries, and some ethnic Lao and Khmer joined the Vietminh to cooperate in the struggle to overthrow French rule. Paradoxically, however, the rise of revolutionary sentiment coincided with a growing sense of national and ethnic awareness in the two protectorates, and some Lao and Khmer evidently criticized Vietnamese domination over the movement. Party leaders responded at the Second Congress in 1951 by splitting the ICP into three separate national organizations—the

---

[29] The Comintern reasoned that revolutionary movements in small countries could succeed only if they coalesced into large federations. Whether or not strategists in Moscow were aware of the cultural differences among the three societies is unknown. In any case, they felt that the shared experience of exploitation at the hands of French colonialism was adequate justification for cooperation. The Vietnamese soon fell into line. According to a resolution issued by the new ICP Central Committee in October 1930, to leave the workers in Cambodia and Laos out of the new party would be incorrect, because although the three nations were distinctive in language, customs, and race, they were united by their political and economic circumstances. See "An nghi quyet cua TU toan the hoi nghi noi ve tinh hinh hien tai o Dong Duong" [Resolution of the plenary Central Committee on the current situation in Indochina], in *Lich su Dang Cong San Viet Nam: trich van kien dang* [A history of the Vietnamese Communist Party: selected party documents] (Hanoi: Publishing House for Texts on Marxism-Leninism, 1979), p. 60. Also see Huynh Kim Khanh, pp. 128–129, and my *The Communist Road*, p. 142, for discussion and reference.

VWP and the so-called People's Revolutionary Party in both Laos and Cambodia. The change was primarily cosmetic, for internal party documents made it clear that the Vietnamese would continue to play a guiding role in the movement. Some documents even suggested the formation of a united party and federation after the eviction of the French colonial regime.[30]

At Geneva, DRV negotiators demanded that delegates from the revolutionary movements in Laos and Cambodia be formally seated at the conference. The Western powers refused, however, claiming that neither movement possessed substantial popular support, and recognized only representatives of the two royal governments of Laos and Cambodia which the French had established a few months previously. At first, China supported the Vietnamese demands, but in June Zhou Enlai shifted his stance and pressured the DRV to accept the French position. In early July, Zhou held a private talk with Ho Chi Minh near the Sino-Vietnamese border. At that meeting, Ho apparently gave in. He also agreed to a statement that Vietnamese relations with Laos and Cambodia should be characterized by the five principles of peaceful coexistence. To sweeten Ho's assent, China may have promised to support Vietnam's struggle for reunification, and an aid agreement was signed shortly afterward.[31]

Were China's actions at the Geneva Conference motivated by its desire to weaken Vietnam and promote Chinese domination over Indochina? At this point, the evidence is insufficient to provide a definitive answer. One reason for Zhou's behavior at the conference may have been China's desire to improve relations with the neutralist government of Prime Minister Nehru in India. According to the French scholar François Joyaux, Chinese

---

[30] Duiker, *The Communist Road,* p. 143. The exact moment for the demise of the Indochinese Federation remains obscure. According to a document on the Indochinese Federation issued by Hanoi in April 1978, the concept was not raised after February 1951, the date of the decision to form three separate revolutionary organizations. See "Document on Indochina Federation," VNA, April 17, 1978, cited in Foreign Broadcast Information Service (FBIS), vol. 4, K12–13. Other Vietnamese sources, however, suggest that the idea was dropped after the formation of three separate states in 1953 and 1954. For a somewhat sanitized version of events from Hanoi's perspective, see Nguyen Van Nhat, "Tinh doan ket chien dau chong ke thu chung cua nhan dan ba nuoc Dong Duong tu 1945 toi nay" [The spirit of unified struggle against the common enemy of the three Indochinese peoples from 1945 until today], NCLS, January 1981.

[31] For a discussion of the meeting, see Joyaux, pp. 263–264.

policy at Geneva was influenced to a considerable degree by the desire to please Nehru who, despite his public gestures of support for the Vietminh, apparently hoped to keep all of Indochina from falling entirely under the domination of the Vietnamese communists.[32] This is plausible, since it coincides with China's desire to improve relations with India and improve its standing among neutralist nations in the Third World. But there is reason to believe that Beijing, as Hanoi suspects, was also acting in its own interests when it supported the consolidation of neutralist noncommunist governments in Laos and Cambodia. Chinese leaders were undoubtedly aware of previous Vietnamese plans for creating an Indochinese Federation, and could not have been especially pleased at the prospect, which undercut Beijing's effort to build a protective belt of neutralist states free of imperialist control along its southern frontier. Not only would the alleged DRV plan for an Indochinese Federation appear to rule out a meaningful role for the PRC in the area, it might also provoke a strong counterresponse from the Western powers and embroil the region once more in a Cold War crisis. In sum, while there is no concrete evidence that Beijing deliberately sought to maintain a division of Vietnam, it does seem possible that it did pressure the Vietnamese to abandon, or at least to modify, their future plans for Indochina. Ho's commitment to Zhou that the relations among the three states would be characterized by the "five principles" suggests, at least by implication, that Zhou may have exacted a price on Indochina in return for continued Chinese assistance to the Vietnamese.[33]

Hanoi's claim that China acted in its own interest and sacrificed those of the Vietnamese revolution at Geneva thus seem justified. That should not occasion surprise. In subordinating the interests of their smaller ally to their own policy requirements, the Chinese were following well-worn precedent. On several occasions in the 1930s and 1940s, the USSR had

---

[32] Joyaux, p. 249. Nehru may also have played a role in persuading Zhou to accept a delay in national elections in Vietnam. See ibid., p. 252.

[33] Tao Bingwei, director of the Asian-Pacific Office at the Institute for International Studies in Beijing, insists that at that time China had no suspicion of Vietnamese plans to dominate Indochina. Interview with Tao Bingwei, Institute for International Studies, August 13, 1985. Another Chinese official privately informed me, however, that in his view China was indeed concerned at that time of Vietnamese plans to form a federation with Laos and Cambodia.

sacrificed the immediate needs of nonruling Asian communist parties (including the ICP) to the shifting requirements of Soviet foreign policy in Europe. A generation later, Hanoi itself imposed a policy of moderation on the revolutionary parties of Laos and Cambodia in order to further its own strategy interests in South Vietnam.[34] The fact is, where the interests of the larger power conflicted with those of a smaller ally, the needs of the latter have been invariably sacrificed. There are sometimes valid reasons for this difference in perspective, since the former is often forced to operate in a larger foreign policy framework which the latter, in its single-minded focus on the imperatives of purely local concerns, does not, or chooses not, to recognize. At Geneva, the concerns of the Vietnamese were sacrificed, not only by the Chinese, but by the Soviet Union as well, as the global powers attempted to retreat from the precipice of global confrontation over Indochina and find grounds for a new era of peaceful coexistence.

Conclusions

The Geneva Conference, then, resulted in a settlement that in many respects was unsatisfactory to the leaders of the DRV. Lacking the power to do otherwise, and needing the support of Moscow and Beijing, the Vietnamese had no recourse but to accept the solution. In private, however, some Vietnamese officials complained bitterly that they had been betrayed by their larger allies. Today Hanoi, more outspoken, contends that Vietminh forces could have liberated all of Indochina after the fall of Dien Bien Phu had China been willing to provide additional military support. China, however, apparently refused such support for fear of widening the conflict. That, Hanoi now claims, was a specious argument. The French were in disarray and the route to Hanoi was open. As for the United States, it had been profoundly shaken by its experience in Korea and was reluctant to become involved in another conflict on the Asian mainland.

---

[34] There is, of course, room for disagreement on the merits of such policies. Were the actions of the larger power taken in the overall interests of world revolution, or in the narrower interest of national security or territorial aggrandizement? Given the difficulty of attempting to sort out ideological and national components in the foreign policy of each country, there is little point in seeking to find an answer.

China has retorted that the Vietminh were not in a position to win a total military victory and that in 1965 Pham Van Dong had conceded as much, commenting to Mao Zedong that the battle of Dien Bien Phu "could only liberate half of our homeland."[35]

Here, perhaps, the Chinese have the better of the argument. While it is not unlikely that the Vietminh, with substantial material assistance from the PRC, could have overrun the demoralized French forces in the Red River Delta, a total victory over the entire country at that point was problematic. Without respect to the question of whether the Vietminh forces were in a position after Dien Bien Phu to launch an offensive on the Red River Delta (and Nikita Khrushchev, for one, strongly suggests that they were not), their position in the South was considerably weaker, and they would have encountered serious logistical problems in supplying a major operation there. More important, perhaps, the threat of a Vietminh takeover by force of the entire country (or even the Red River Delta) or a breakdown in the Geneva talks, would almost certainly have provoked a strong military reaction from the Eisenhower Administration, which had already drawn up contingency plans for the introduction of U.S. troops into Indochina. Ho Chi Minh, at least, appeared to understand the problem. At the plenary session of the Central Committee in July, he noted that some members of the party who wanted to continue the struggle did not see the United States beyond the French. While Ho's comments may have been aimed at justifying the decision to accept a settlement to bitter southerners who felt that they had been sold out at Geneva, it is more likely that Ho, with a deeper sense of the international situation than his colleagues, was warning party militants to accept reality.[36]

Whatever the final judgment on such matters, it is clear that the Geneva Conference exerted a significant impact on Sino-Vietnamese relations and contributed to a growing sense of bitterness and distrust on both sides. While the disagreements that had emerged at the conference were papered over in the

---

[35] *The Truth*, p. 14. The Chinese response was given in *Beijing Review*, November 23 and 30, 1979.

[36] For Ho's comments, and a discussion of the issues involved, see my *The Communist Road*, p. 163.

interests of avoiding a split, the growing tension in the relationship promised to bring a new complexity to the always complicated relations between the two countries.

III

Beijing, Hanoi, and the Second Indochina War

The Geneva Accords resulted in the de facto division of Vietnam into two separate states, with the DRV in the North and a non-Communist regime supported by the United States in the South. Although the settlement had made provisions for national elections to be held in 1956, the political protocol that provided for such arrangements was ambiguous in wording and lacked teeth to guarantee enforcement. In Laos the Vietminh-supported revolutionary movement had been granted a small regroupment zone consisting of two provinces in the northern part of the country, but the royal government with its capital in Vientiane was recognized as the legitimate government of Laos. In Cambodia the insurgency movement received nothing.

In the months following the conclusion of the conference, both China and the DRV moved rapidly to repair their mutual ties and defuse potential sources of tension in their relationship. Both countries, indeed, had good reason to do so. Hanoi would need Chinese assistance, both to stimulate economic development in the North and to pursue the course of national reunification in the South. Chinese support would be especially critical in view of the fact that the post-Stalinist leadership in the USSR had made it clear that it had little interest in promoting the cause of the Vietnamese revolution.

China had its own reasons for wanting to improve ties between the two countries. Although the Geneva agreement had reduced the likelihood of a direct Sino-U.S. confrontation, the formation of the U.S.-sponsored Southeast Asia Treaty Organization (SEATO) in September and the growing American presence in South Vietnam indicated that the threat of imperialism to China's southern frontier had by no means subsided. While

Chinese leaders clearly hoped to avoid a resumption of the Indochina conflict, they undoubtedly viewed the DRV as the keystone of their national security perimeter in Southeast Asia.

The main obstacle to good relations between the two countries was the issue of the resumption of war in Vietnam. For the immediate future, however, this issue did not present a potential source of conflict, since Vietnamese leaders recognized the need to concentrate their immediate attention on building a firm base in the North and assuring the holding of national elections throughout the country, in accordance with the provisions of the Geneva Accords.[1] Yet there were a number of other potentially divisive issues in the relationship. One source of possible disagreement was the question of the Sino-Vietnamese frontier. The existing border between China and Vietnam, like that between China and its other neighbors in South and Southeast Asia, had been established during the colonial period at a time of Chinese weakness. The land border between China and Vietnam had been established by treaties between France and the Qing dynasty signed in 1887 and 1895. A few years later France ceded adjacent areas to China in exchange for trade rights and consulates in China. These accords had also established a border in the Gulf of Tonkin that established ownership over a series of small offshore islands.[2]

Possible differences over the land border at the time appeared to be a matter of relatively little significance. The area of disagreement involved only a few square kilometers of territory

---

[1] There is no evidence of any disagreement within the VWP leadership over the question of priorities in the immediate post-Geneva period. The question of reunification elections, however, may have been a source of concern. It is not clear whether Hanoi expected the elections to take place, although it behaved publicly as if it anticipated that they would be held. The Chinese were apparently more cynical about the matter, and reportedly told the Vietnamese that there would be no elections, so they should prepare for a protracted war. See *Beijing Review,* December 7, 1979.

[2] A brief statement of the historical background from the Vietnamese point of view can be found in the "Memorandum on Chinese Provocations and Territorial Encroachments upon Vietnamese Territory," *Vietnam News Bulletin* (April 10, 1979). For a more recent analysis, see Minh Nghia, "The Legal Foundation of the Border Line between Vietnam and China," *Vietnam Courier* (July 1985), pp. 26–27. China's view is presented in the "Memo on Vice President Li Xiannian's Talks with Premier Pham Van Dong," reported in *People's Daily,* March 23, 1979.

with limited economic value. At the time of the original Sino-French agreements, border stones had been laid out to demarcate the boundary, but they were often placed several kilometers apart, leaving the precise border subject to local interpretations. Because the land border did not follow natural geographical features such as rivers or mountain ridges, local disagreements inevitably arose over the precise boundary. Many of the disputes stemmed from issues of local economic importance, such as the use of waterways or trails, fishing rights or pasture lands.

After the conclusion of the Geneva Conference and the return of the DRV to Hanoi, local authorities on both sides of the border held discussions aimed at resolving such disagreements. After several unsuccessful efforts, the issue was referred to the central governments. In 1958 the Central Committee of each ruling Communist Party agreed to maintain the status quo for the time being to avoid a squabble and instructed that all future disputes concerning the land border should be resolved through negotiations at the central government level.

The problem of the sea boundary was of relatively little immediate importance, but potentially more complicated. The Sino-French accords of 1887 and 1895 had delineated the coastal boundary between the Protectorate of Tonkin and the Chinese province of Gwangdong at 108 degrees, 03 minutes, and 18 seconds, Greenwich. Because at that time territorial waters were based on the principle of the three-mile offshore limit, the demarcation was undertaken primarily for the purpose of establishing ownership over small islands off the coast, and the gulf itself was apparently not mentioned by name in the text.

The same ambiguity existed over the final territorial question between the two nations—ownership over the Paracel and Spratly Islands in the South China Sea, a question that had not been dealt with in the Sino-French negotiations at the end of the nineteenth century. The historical record relating to ownership of both island clusters was particularly ambiguous. Tiny in size (most were mere sand spits and atolls), they possessed little apparent economic value and had been occupied only sporadically in the precolonial era. Historical records later presented by both governments supported claims that both the Chinese and Vietnamese empires had at one time or another discovered and administered islands in both groups. Neither, however, had ever placed permanent settlements on the islands. Moreover, the documents themselves were vague, and subject to differing interpretations. The Spratly Islands, in particular, were so spread out that different islands could have been occupied and administered by more than one claimant at a given time.[3]

Of the two, the Paracels had the most active history. China has recently cited historical records to claim that they had been discovered by a Chinese naval flotilla during the period of the Three Kingdoms, in the early Christian era. At various times, according to such documents, the islands were administered and occupied by China. In the early twentieth century an admiral of the Chinese fleet paid a brief inspection visit to confirm Chinese ownership. According to Beijing, the first challenge to Chinese sovereignty came from the French after the establishment of their protectorate over North and Central Vietnam in the late nineteenth century. At first France had appeared to accept Chinese claims over the islands. But the discovery of guano (useful for the manufacture of artificial fertilizer) gave the islands an economic value, and in the early 1930s France occupied some of them, asserting that documents in the Vietnamese imperial archives indicated prior ownership by the Vietnamese empire. The Chinese government, then under Chiang Kai-shek, issued a protest against French occupation but took no military action. During the Pacific War, the Paracels were occupied by the Japanese. After the surrender of Japan, some of the islands were briefly occupied by forces of the Republic of China. In 1950 they were replaced by military units of the new Communist mainland regime, and in succeeding years Beijing attempted to consolidate its rule by colonizing them with settlers from Hainan Island and constructing a military base on Yung Xing Island. Other islands, however, we reoccupied by the French until their departure from Indochina in 1954. A few years later the Saigon regime seized several of the unoccupied islands and operated a small enterprise to quarry phosphate fertilizer.

The case of the Spratlys is equally complex. More isolated and of less apparent economic value than the Paracels, the Sprat-

---

[3] The claims of the two governments and the history of the issue can be found in *Vietnam News Bulletin* (April 10, 1979) and in "China's Indisputable Sovereignty over the Xisha and Nansha Islands," *Beijing Review,* February 18, 1980. For an analysis, see Justus M. van der Kroef, "The South China Sea: Competing Claims and Strategic Conflicts," *International Security Review* vol. 7, no. 3 (Fall 1982).

lys were rarely inhabited during the premodern period, and served mainly as a base for pirates, although they were claimed by China. During the 1930s several were occupied by the French, who constructed a meterological station on Itu Aba. They were seized by Japan in the early 1940s, but after the war the French returned. Itu Aba, however, was occupied by military units of the Republic of China. When the French abandoned the area after the Geneva Conference, the Saigon regime occupied three of the islands.

In the years immediately following the Geneva Accords, the sea boundary and the islands did not emerge as a major issue in Sino-Vietnamese relations. In early September 1958 Prime Minister Zhou Enlai wrote a letter to the DRV on the issue. In the note Zhou stated that China's territorial sea was twelve nautical miles and included the islands of Xisha and Nansha (the Chinese names for the Paracels and Spratlys respectively). A few days later Vietnamese Prime Minister Pham Van Dong replied. His reply was somewhat ambiguous, stating only that the DRV recognized and supported the declaration of the PRC on Chinese territorial waters. There was no mention of the islands although, according to Chinese sources, in later years Vietnamese maps listed the islands as Chinese. For the moment, the two regimes had clearly tacitly agreed to set the issue aside.[4]

The Overseas Chinese

A second issue fraught with the potential for disturbing Sino-Vietnamese relations was that of the ethnic Chinese residing in Vietnam. Numbering more than two million in 1954, most were descendants of settlers who had emigrated from China generations earlier. Some had been assimilated into Vietnamese society, but most retained their Chinese nationality and culture, attended Chinese schools, and spoke the Chinese language. The majority lived in the southern provinces, although there were between 100,000 and 200,000 in the North. Most were merchants, but some Chinese in the North were fishermen, miners, stevedores, and farmers.

Traditionally, the Chinese government had followed a policy of *jus sanguinus* (the law of blood) and asserted its sovereignty over Chinese nationals living abroad. In the years following the

---

[4] The letters were published in *Beijing Review,* March 30, 1979.

end of World War II, however, this policy had created difficulties with newly independent governments in Southeast Asia, and in the mid-1950s, in an attempt to allay such concerns, the PRC reached agreements with several Southeast Asian countries, according to which Chinese nationals in such countries were encouraged to adopt local citizenship. This formed a pattern for Chinese negotiations with the DRV. In 1955 talks between the central committees of both parties resulted in an agreement by which the PRC agreed that all subjects of Chinese origin living in the DRV should be encouraged to assimilate on a voluntary and gradual basis into Vietnamese society. In return, the DRV agreed not to discriminate against those who refused. In succeeding years, Hanoi kept its promise. Ethnic Chinese were permitted, if they so chose, to retain Chinese citizenship and their own schools. Despite the overall policy calling for nationalization of commerce and industry, a small private sector, dominated by Chinese merchants, continued to operate in the cities. When war broke out in the South, the Chinese were not subject to the draft, although they were encouraged to volunteer for military service.[5]

Chinese Assistance and the Maoist Model

In the years immediately following the Geneva Conference, both China and North Vietnam had moved expeditiously to set their mutual relationship on a firm and fraternal footing. Both sides made liberal use of symbolism. In June 1955 President Ho Chi Minh, always careful to cultivate his Chinese colleagues, led the first official DRV delegation to Beijing amidst mutual protestations of eternal friendship. Mao Zedong publicly disavowed Chinese mistreatment of Vietnam during the feudal period, and when Premier Zhou Enlai visited Hanoi in November 1956, he laid a bouquet of flowers at the altar of the Nhi Chinh Temple in an expression of respect for the rebellion launched in A.D. 39 against Chinese rule.[6]

---

[5] For a recent analysis of Chinese policy toward the ethnic Chinese living in Southeast Asia, see Leo Suryadinata, *China and the ASEAN States: The Ethnic Chinese Dimension* (Kent Ridge: Singapore University Press, 1985).

[6] "The Truth about Sino-Vietnamese Relations," *Guoji wenti yanjiu* [Studies in International Problems], no. 2 (October 1981), trans. in JPRS 79,661.

Another visible manifestation of improving mutual relations showed in the rising level of Chinese economic assistance to the Hanoi regime. As noted above, the two sides had reached agreement on an aid pact during the Geneva Conference. According to one U.S. source, by 1961 China had provided more than $600 million in assistance to the DRV, considerably more than that donated by the Soviet Union.[7] In return, the Hanoi regime continued to rely on the Chinese developmental model. It adopted the Maoist concept of New Democracy (according to which the transition to socialism should be delayed until political consolidation and economic growth had been achieved) as its overall strategical guideline for the immediate post-Geneva period. Agricultural policy, administrative organization, and the training of cadres and party members all followed Chinese patterns, and in 1957 the DRV adopted its own version of the "Hundred Flowers" program in the PRC.[8]

It soon became evident, however, that the "Chinese road to socialism" had mixed results when applied to Vietnam. The Chinese land reform program, which involved a high level of class struggle in the villages, aroused considerable discontent in North Vietnam and was eventually scaled down after a stormy Central Committee meeting in 1956. The Maoist model of cadre training and social mobilization, which was also characterized by a high level of class conflict and a populist distrust of urban elites, was soon seen as inappropriate in Vietnam and was replaced by a more hierarchical model based on the concept of party rule and a stable relationship linking each village with the bureaucracy. In 1958 Hanoi announced that it had no intention of adopting the new Chinese system of communes, and by the beginning of the new decade, the appeal of Chinese experience was clearly on the wane.[9]

---

[7] Jay Taylor, *China and Southeast Asia* (New York: Praeger, 1976), p. 20, fn. 57.

[8] For a discussion, see Georges Boudarel, "l'Idéocratie importée au Vietnam avec le Maoisme," in Georges Boudarel et al., eds., *La Bureaucratie au Vietnam* (Paris: l'Harmattan, 1983).

[9] Georges Boudarel and David W.P. Elliott, "Institutionalizing the Revolution: Vietnam's Search for a Model of Development," in William S. Turley, ed., *Vietnamese Communism in Comparative Perspective* (Boulder, Colo.: Westview Press, 1980), pp. 72–84.

The War in the South

The Hanoi regime had delayed further action on reunification with the South at least partly in the hope that national elections would be held as called for by the Geneva Accords. Hopes for a political settlement grew appreciably dimmer in the summer of 1955, when the Saigon regime under President Ngo Dinh Diem refused to hold consultations with the North on elections. Diem made clear his intention of repressing the revolutionary movement in the South, and took action against Vietminh elements seeking to organize committees to force elections.

Whether or not party leaders in Hanoi had expected the elections to take place—a question that has not been definitely resolved—the breakdown of the Geneva process faced them with a serious dilemma. Hanoi had counted on the continued strength of the revolutionary movement in the South and the weakness of the Diem regime as its main trump cards in the struggle to achieve national reunification by primarily political means. If the political option failed, it would have to resort to an armed struggle. Such a policy, however, would find little favor in either Moscow or Beijing, and might trigger a U.S. response.

In 1956 party leaders in Hanoi, in reaction to the continued repression of party supporters in the South, began to devote increased attention to the possibility of escalating the level of revolutionary struggle there. There is little doubt that one of the regime's primary concerns was the response that such a proposal would elicit in major Communist capitals. Moscow reacted predictably. The Soviet leadership under Nikita Khrushchev remained anxious to avoid confrontation with the United States and attempted to persuade the Vietnamese to abide by the Geneva Accords and seek a peaceful road to national reunification. DRV leaders, themselves divided over the issue, and anxious to retain good relations with Moscow, publicly announced their approval of the new policy of peaceful coexistence; but privately Hanoi began to lobby vigorously for its view that in Vietnam the "peaceful road to socialism" might be a chimera.[10]

---

[10] For analysis, see W.R. Smyser, *The Independent Vietnamese: Vietnamese Communism between Russia and China, 1956–1969* (Athens: Ohio University Press), Southeast Asia Series Number 55, pp. 7–20.

China, however, offered better prospects. In 1957 the PRC moved perceptibly to the Left in both domestic and foreign policy. Internally, Mao Zedong's concern about the decline of revolutionary élan in China led him to seek ways to reinvigorate the party and society. In foreign affairs, the regime moved away from an emphasis on moderation and peaceful coexistence in favor of a more confrontational stance toward the outside world. While there may have been several reasons for the shift, the crisis over Taiwan and the offshore islands appears to have been a critical factor. The buildup of U.S. military power on Taiwan led China to turn for support to Moscow. But Khrushchev refused to promise full support to China in the ensuing Quemoy crisis, thus casting the value of the Soviet alliance into doubt and increasing China's sense of isolation in the international arena.

Beijing reacted by returning full circle to the revolutionary posture that had characterized its foreign policy in 1949. This raised Vietnam once again into the symbol of China's vision of a revolt of the oppressed masses of Asia against the power of global imperialism. As in the early 1950s, however, revolutionary enthusiasm was tempered by realism. When, sometime in 1958, DRV leaders queried Beijing about the advisability of returning to a policy of armed struggle in the South the latter, now increasingly fearful of the risks of possible confrontation with the United States, responded that the time was not yet ripe for a new revolutionary surge in Indochina. The North Vietnamese, said China, should adopt a policy of "prolonged ambush" and await a better opportunity for launching an all-out armed struggle.[11] Hanoi, however, had learned to its cost the dangers of excessive dependence on its larger allies, and while party leaders were anxious to avoid antagonizing either Moscow or Beijing, in the matter of national reunification they were prepared, if necessary, to go it alone. In May 1959, after extensive and perhaps acrimonious deliberations, the Central Committee approved a Politburo proposal to resume revolutionary war in the South.[12] At

---

[11] *The Truth,* pp. 29-33. China now apparently concedes its error in judgment in doubting the chances of success in South Vietnam. See Hoang Van Hoan's comments in *Beijing Review,* December 7, 1979, p. 15.

[12] I have discussed the circumstances surrounding the decision in my *The Communist Road,* pp. 186-190. For Hanoi's version, see *Cuoc khang chien chong my cuu nuoc 1954-1975: nhung su kien quan su* [The anti-U.S. resistance war for national salvation, 1954-1975: military events; hereafter *CKC*] (Hanoi: People's Army Publishing House, 1980), trans. in JPRS 80,968, pp. 28-32. Ac-

first, party leaders were uncertain about the level of armed struggle that might be required to topple the Diem regime and may have hoped that a relatively limited effort would suffice. Such a strategy would have the double advantage of avoiding problems with Moscow and Beijing and reducing the likelihood of direct U.S. intervention in the South. But Diem reacted vigorously to the challenge of the growing revolutionary movement (popularly known as the "Viet Cong"), and in early 1961 Hanoi decided to increase the level of armed violence in the South. In Washington the new Kennedy administration was not slow to respond, and by mid-year had begun to increase the level of U.S. assistance to the Saigon regime.

The escalation of armed conflict in South Vietnam increased Hanoi's dependence upon outside assistance. It did not find it in Moscow. Although Nikita Khrushchev had promised Soviet support for wars of national liberation in a speech given in January 1961, Soviet leaders were unwilling to risk confrontation with Washington over the Vietnam issue and refused to provide firm backing to North Vietnamese activities in the South. At first, Hanoi had little better luck with China. In mid-1960 Chinese leaders reportedly warned the Vietnamese against military escalation in the South.[13] By late 1961, however, the split between the USSR and China had come out into the open, and the latter was determined to demonstrate the sincerity of its support for the cause of world revolution. Hanoi was the prime beneficiary. The level of Chinese assistance to the DRV now began to increase, and the Beijing regime took great pains to stress the historic friendships between the Chinese and Vietnamese peoples.

Chinese assistance, however, had a price. Attempting to take advantage of strained relations between the DRV and the Soviet Union, Beijing pressed Hanoi to take China's side in the Sino-Soviet dispute. In a visit to Hanoi in May 1963, Liu Shao-qi lectured his hosts by remarking that "on questions of such an important struggle of principle, we cannot act as lookers-on or

---

cording to one scholar, Khrushchev's verbal support for wars of national liberation was the result of a compromise reached at the meeting of 81 Communist parties in October 1980. See R.B. Smith, *An International History of the Vietnam War: Revolution vs. Containment 1955-1961* (London: St. Martin's Press, 1983), p. 223.

[13] CKC, pp. 44-45.

follow a middle course." Hanoi has recently charged that Deng Xiaoping offered massive aid to the DRV, but only if the latter refused further assistance from the USSR.[14]

The split placed the DRV in a difficult position. While Hanoi might hope to reap some benefits from the split—namely that Moscow and Beijing might be induced to increase the level of their support as a means of courting Hanoi for its support with the socialist camp—on balance party leaders probably viewed it as a disadvantage to their own cause, since it prevented the formation of a united front of the socialist nations to deter direct U.S. involvement in the Vietnam conflict. It also undercut the sense of unity with the VWP. While there is little evidence that the party leadership itself was seriously split, as was sometimes charged, into pro-Soviet and pro-Chinese factions, Vietnamese sources have conceded that pro-Soviet and pro-Chinese elements did exist within the party as a whole.[15]

The overthrow of the Diem regime by a military coup in November 1963 added a new element of complexity to the situation. It also put additional strains on the vaunted unity within the VWP. Some wanted to take advantage of the chaotic situation in Saigon and seek a quick a victory before the United States could stabilize the situation; others feared a strong U.S. reaction and wanted to retain limits on Northern involvement in the struggle with the South. At a stormy Central Committee plenum held in December the former view prevailed, and the Hanoi regime decided to dispatch regular forces of the North Vietnamese Army into the South in preparation for a general offensive to seize power in Saigon. Sensitive to the possibility of a hostile reaction in Moscow and Beijing, the party sent a circular letter to socialist capitals explaining the decision and predicting that the United States would not intervene. If it did, Hanoi promised that the conflict could be limited to South Vietnam.[16]

---

[14] *The Truth*, p. 33

[15] A reference to the existence of a pro-Soviet "revisionist" faction in the VWP can be found in William S. Turley, *Interviews with PAVN and LDP Defectors: Officers, Men and Political Cadres* (Carbondale: Southern Illinois University Press, 1974), vol. I, pp. 93–100. References to "Maoist" influence in the party have been common in the official press since the end of the war. See, for example, Le Duc Tho's address on party building at the Fifth National Congress in the spring of 1982, trans. in FBIS, *Asia and the Pacific*, April 8, 1982.

[16] Duiker, *The Communist Road*, p. 225; CKC, pp. 55–56.

The response in Beijing would be of particular importance, for DRV leaders were undoubtedly counting on the threat of direct Chinese intervention to deter the United States from entering the conflict.

As Hanoi had probably anticipated, the reaction to the new strategy was cool in Moscow, although Soviet leaders did make a vague gesture of support. China, too, was cautious. A *People's Daily* editorial published in late December—and perhaps reacting to the decisions made at the VWP plenum—appeared to urge that the revolutionary movement in the South could achieve victory without an escalation of the war or the introduction of regular forces from the North.[17] Chinese leaders were undoubtedly concerned that the Vietnamese, in their single-minded pursuit of national reunification, could draw China into a direct confrontation with the United States. There were indications in the DRV official press that Hanoi indeed counted on Chinese support in such a contingency. An article in the January issue of the party's theoretical journal, *Hoc Tap,* declared that if the United States invaded the North, it would have to contend not only with the forces of the DRV, but also with those of China. A few weeks later, responding to reports that the Johnson administration was considering air strikes against targets in North Vietnam, Hanoi replied that "together with the strength of the peoples and armed forces of the friendly countries in the socialist camp—which support us closely—our strength is second to none."[18]

China tried to reassure its ally of its support while at the same time avoiding inflammatory statements that might fuel the growing crisis. During the spring and early summer Western intelligence sources reported a buildup of Chinese armed forces in China's southern provinces, and in July Foreign Minister Chen I (Ch'en Yi), in a letter to his counterpart in Hanoi, assured the latter that "China and the DRV are friends and neighbors like lips and teeth. The Chinese people cannot be expected to look on with folded arms in the face of any aggression against the DRV." Chen I did not allude to the conditions that would bring

---

[17] *People's Daily,* December 20, 1963, cited in Eugene K. Lawson, *The Sino-Vietnamese Conflict* (New York: Praeger, 1984), p. 28.

[18] *Quan doi nhan dan* [People's army], March 3, 1964, as cited in "CIA Secret Report on Sino-Vietnamese Reaction to American Tactics in the Vietnamese War," *Journal of Contemporary Asia,* vol. 13, no. 2 (1983), p. 261. Hereafter, CIA report.

China directly into the conflict.[19]

Chinese leaders may have hoped that such statements would deter the United States from steps that might further inflame the crisis, but the Tonkin Gulf incident in early August and U.S. bombing raids on military targets in the North showed that the Johnson administration was prepared to take further military action in Indochina. If anything, however, U.S. action made Beijing more cautious. While reiterating Chinese support for the DRV, China informed the United States through private channels that it would make a "patient and moderate" response to the air strikes. By fall, Chinese officials had begun to imply that China would only intervene directly if the United States invaded North Vietnam. Early the following year, Mao Zedong reportedly went even further, informing American journalist Edgar Snow that China would only enter the war if the United States attacked the Chinese mainland.[20]

For Hanoi, the Chinese reaction was undoubtedly a disappointment. It had clearly counted on the threat of Chinese involvement as a deterrent to U.S. intervention in the conflict, and the wary response in Beijing provoked one Vietnamese official to remark that when the United States attacked the DRV "the Soviets did nothing and the Chinese only talked." Hanoi would later charge that by making clear its conditions, Beijing released the Johnson administration from concern about the consequences of a possible decision to engage in limited war in South Vietnam.[21]

The overthrow of Nikita Khrushchev in October 1964 brought new complexity to the situation. It was clearly a boon to Hanoi, for the new Soviet leadership under Leonid Brezhnev quickly showed a greater willingness than its predecessor to help the Vietnamese. While Moscow was still determined to avoid a confrontation with the United States, it appeared more willing to

---

[19] Ibid., p. 264.

[20] Ibid., p. 265.

[21] *The Truth,* pp. 35–36. There may be some justice in this contention. In 1970, ex-President Johnson said that he had been reluctant to ask for a formal declaration of war against North Vietnam because of the possibility it might bring China and the USSR into the conflict. Even after Beijing had made its reluctance to intervene known to the United States, however, it is likely that Washington was deterred from strong action by the fear of Chinese intervention. See Jay Taylor, pp. 32–35.

aid its friends around the world—thus confronting the challenge posed by the message of radicalism in Beijing. By early 1965, Moscow was promising an increase in assistance to the DRV in return for a serious Vietnamese effort to promote a peace settlement.

The shift in Moscow brought new problems for Beijing. By demonstrating a new willingness to provide assistance to its Third World allies, the Brezhnev leadership undercut China's contention that only the PRC was sincerely devoted to promoting the fortunes of the smaller countries in the socialist camp. In mid-February China's Vietnam strategy suffered another blow when the Johnson administration, in response to a Viet Cong attack on a U.S. base camp at Pleiku, initiated a program of systematic bombing of the North and began to introduce U.S. combat forces into South Vietnam. Moscow quickly appealed for "united action" by the socialist countries to assist the DRV and requested an air corridor and the use of air fields in China in order to send military assistance to its beleaguered ally.

The Soviet move was an astute one, since it posed little risk to the Soviet Union while placing China on the defensive. The Beijing regime viewed the conflict in Vietnam primarily in terms of its larger interests, and specifically its relations with the Soviet Union and the United States. It had helped the Vietnamese enough to keep Hanoi from leaning toward the Soviet Union, but not so much as to risk war. The new developments obliged China to demonstrate in more concrete terms the sincerity of its pledges to support the national liberation struggle in Vietnam, thus significantly increasing the risk of confrontation with the United States. Beijing's dilemma over how to react provoked a serious split within a party leadership already badly divided on domestic policy issues. Some, like Liu Shaoqi and CCP General Secretary Deng Xiaoping, continued to see the United States as the main threat to Chinese security and reportedly proposed a limited rapprochement with the Soviet Union to provide joint assistance to the DRV and deter Washington from further escalation of the war. Others, like Mao Zedong himself and Defense Minister Lin Biao (Lin Piao), viewed the split with the USSR as the matter of first priority and argued for a rejection of united action with Moscow.[22]

---

[22] For reasons of space, the debate in Beijing over Chinese involvement in the war cannot be discussed in detail here. In any case, it is treated competently in a

Significantly, the argument revolved more around relations with the Great Powers than about the level of aid that should be sent to the DRV or the strategy that the latter should adopt in South Vietnam. There was probably general agreement that China should continue to assist the DRV, but that such aid should not lead to the risk of general war in Asia. There was probably also a consensus that the struggle in South Vietnam should remain at the level of a protracted war. Despite the Soviet challenge, then, the Chinese leaders kept their involvement in Vietnam under clear limitations. In April VWP General Secretary Le Duan visited Beijing to request Chinese support forces and some combat personnel, including volunteer pilots. According to Chinese sources, an agreement to this effect was signed. At the same time, however, China began to signal its desire to avoid a confrontation with the United States. Although Beijing took a relatively bold line in public, it took no direct action to counter the U.S. military escalation in the South and informed Washington in mid-April that Beijing would not send combat forces to North Vietnam so long as South Vietnamese or American troops did not cross the seventeenth parallel.[23]

During the summer of 1965 China adhered to its cautious policy in Vietnam. In July the PRC reportedly turned down the North Vietnamese request for pilots, arguing that the time was not ripe and that the action would not in any case deter the United States from continuing its air strikes. In early September Defense Minister Lin Biao published an article that in elliptical terms called on the North Vietnamese to practice self-reliance and adopt a strategy of protracted war in the South. Two months later China formally rejected Moscow's appeal for "united action" to provide assistance to the DRV, thus signaling the victory of the Maoist faction in the interparty debate over foreign policy.[24]

China's actions met with little favor in Hanoi, where party planners had decided that an offensive strategy imposing heavy casualties on the battlefield would eventually wear down support for the war in the United States and lead to an American with-

---

number of other sources. See Jay Taylor, chap. 1, and Donald Zagoria, *The Vietnam Triangle: Moscow, Peking, Hanoi* (New York: Pegasus, 1967).

[23] CIA report, p. 269.
[24] Jay Taylor, p. 52; Smyser, p. 92.

drawal. Party leaders gave final approval to the new strategy at a Central Committee plenum in December. With assurances of support from the Soviet Union, and few fears of further escalation by the United States, the DRV now had greater room to maneuver, and no longer felt itself hostage to Chinese assistance. The regime responded sharply to the gratuitous advice emanating from Beijing and attempted to justify its decision to adopt the new strategy. In May 1966 Le Duan remarked in a speech at an army conference that

> it is not fortuitous that in the history of our country, each time we rose to oppose foreign aggression, we took the offensive and not the defensive.... Taking the offensive is a strategy, while taking the defensive is only a strategem. Since the day the South Vietnamese people rose up, they have continually taken the offensive.[25]

The crisis of 1965 represented a turning point in Sino-Vietnamese relations. From now on, Hanoi would rely to an increasing degree on material assistance from the Soviet Union, while China would look with increasing disfavor on the war strategy followed by the North Vietnamese. Neither side was willing to push the dispute to the breaking point, and during the remainder of the decade, the PRC continued to provide substantial amounts of material assistance to the DRV. Chinese sources claim that from October 1965 until March 1967 China sent over 320,000 support forces to provide air defense and engineering, railroad and logistical assistance, as well as substantial amounts of military equipment, including a number of MiG-15s and -17s. Total Chinese aid averaged about U.S.$200 million annually.[26]

But Beijing had clearly imposed limits on the level of its support for the DRV, and according to some observers may now have reached a tacit understanding with the United States to avoid the danger of a direct confrontation. China continued to react strongly to any signs of escalation of the conflict, and reportedly opposed Hanoi's plans for a major offensive in the South in early 1968.[27] According to one source with connections

---

[25] The speech appears in an English version in Zagoria, appendix.

[26] For an estimate of Chinese aid to the DRV, see Jay Taylor, p. 58, and *Beijing Review*. For a report expressing doubt that 300,000 Chinese served in the DRV, see the *Washington Post,* July 31, 1979.

[27] Jay Taylor, p. 61. China has denied this charge and stated that Mao had recommended the launching of a large-scale annihilation campaign to Ho Chi Minh when the latter was in China for medical treatment. See *Beijing Review,* November 30, 1979, p. 14. For evidence that Beijing had reached an understand-

in Hanoi, anger over Chinese attitudes may have led to a rising sentiment within the Vietnamers party leadership to abandon the policy of neutrality in the Sino-Soviet dispute and ally directly with Moscow. This inclination reportedly grew stronger after the death of Ho Chi Minh and the emergence of General Secretary Le Duan as the leading political figure in the party in September 1969.[28]

Crisis over Cambodia

In 1970 a new source of tension was added to the already troubled Sino-Vietnamese relationship when a coup d'etat threw the neutralist Prince Sihanouk out of office and brought a new pro-Western government to power in Cambodia. During the 1950s and 1960s Hanoi and Beijing had engaged in a delicate balancing act over Cambodia. Both, in their own interests, had attempted to maintain good relations with the Sihanouk regime. For China, Sihanouk served as a useful link in the *cordon sanitaire* that it was attempting to create as a means of limiting the imperialist threat to its southern frontier. Sihanouk, an ardent nationalist, also represented a potential buffer against future Vietnamese efforts to dominate Indochina.[29] So the Chinese had attempted to cater to Sihanouk's susceptibilities and support his

---

ing with Washington, see Frank E. Rogers, "Sino-Vietnamese Relations and the Vietnam War, 1965–1966," *China Quarterly,* no. 66 (April 1976). According to a French source, China agreed to stay out of the war if the United States did not attack China, invade North Vietnam, or bomb the dikes. See the *New York Times,* January 16, 1967, cited in Lawson, p. 141.

[28] Truong Nhu Tang, *Vietcong Memoir: An Inside Account of the Vietnam War and its Aftermath* (San Diego: Harcourt Brace Jovanovich, 1985), p. 248. According to Tang, the advocates of a Soviet alliance were Le Duan and Le Duc Tho. Other party leaders such as Vo Nguyen Giap, Truong Chinh, and Pham Van Dong had reservations about a close identification with Moscow.

[29] I have been unable to obtain independent confirmation in Beijing that Chinese leaders viewed Sihanouk as an instrument to control Vietnamese influence in Cambodia. Mr. Tao Bingwei, for example, denies such an assumption and asserts that China did not suspect Hanoi's intentions there until 1975. Interview with Tao Bingwei, Institute for International Studies, Beijing, August 13, 1985. I am still convinced that this motive existed, however. For useful summaries of Chinese policy toward Cambodia, see Melvin Gurtov, *China and Southeast Asia: The Politics of Survival* (Baltimore, MD.: Johns Hopkins Press, 1971), chap. 3; and J.D. Armstrong, *Revolutionary Diplomacy: Chinese Foreign Policy and the United Front Doctrine* (Berkeley and Los Angeles: University of California Press, 1977), chap. 6.

effort to keep Cambodia out of the East-West struggle in Southeast Asia. At the Bandung Conference in 1954 Zhou Enlai had met Sihanouk and given vocal support to Cambodian independence. In the late 1950s leaders of the two countries periodically exchanged state visits, resulting in a treaty of friendship and economic assistance and Cambodian recognition of the PRC as the legitimate government of China. The relationship was not without its problems. China was critical of Sihanouk's decision to accept military assistance from the U.S. in 1955 and, after Beijing's shift to the left in 1957, of his refusal to break diplomatic ties with the United States. In turn, Sihanouk (whose primary immediate concern was to protect Cambodia's borders from the irredentist demands of neighboring South Vietnam and Thailand) was irritated at China's refusal to make a blanket guarantee of Cambodian territorial integrity.[30]

To Hanoi, Sihanouk was useful for another reason. North Vietnamese policy in the late 1950s and early 1960s relied to a considerable degree on the use of Cambodia's eastern provinces as a sanctuary for its revolutionary forces in South Vietnam. Sihanouk, anxious to avoid antagonizing Hanoi, granted its forces tacit permission to operate in the area, while vigorously denying to the United States and the South Vietnamese the right of hot pursuit. In turn, the DRV supported Cambodian neutralism and instructed the pro-Hanoi leadership of the small Kampuchean People's Revolutionary Party (KPRP) not to initiate armed struggle against the Phnom Penh regime.

Sihanouk was not blind to the potential threat posed by his Communist neighbors and, in his circuitous fashion, attempted to balance Hanoi and Beijing against each other. In the early 1960s he sought a statement guaranteeing Cambodian territorial integrity from both countries and induced China to convene a meeting of both countries in Beijing for that purpose. At first, negotiations stalled because of Hanoi's refusal to provide specific guarantees and Beijing's unwillingness to antagonize the North Vietnamese by siding with Cambodia. In 1967, at a time of increasing Viet Cong activity in the eastern provinces, Sihanouk raised the issue again and obtained additional, if still ambiguous, guarantees of Cambodian national frontiers.[31]

---

[30] Armstrong, p. 191.

[31] Gurtov, *China and Southeast Asia*, p. 67; Armstrong, p. 206. For a statement regarding the importance to Hanoi of the sanctuary in Cambodia, see

The delicate fabric of mutual accommodation over Cambodia gradually began to unravel during the late 1960s. In 1963 a dissident faction of the KPRP led by Paris-trained radical nationalists under the leadership of Pol Pot (real name Saloth Sar) wrested power within the party from pro-Hanoi elements. Suspicious of Hanoi's long-term intentions in Cambodia and convinced that the existing policy of accommodation with Sihanouk served Vietnamese and not Khmer interests, the new leadership renamed the organization the Kampuchean Communist Party (KCP) and in 1968, after the return of Pol Pot from a visit to Beijing, launched an armed insurrection against the Sihanouk regime.[32]

Sihanouk, already irritated at the increasing Vietnamese presence in Cambodia's eastern provinces, apparently began to turn once more to the United States. According to Henry Kissinger, Sihanouk privately sanctioned the secret bombing of the sanctuaries ordered by the Nixon administration, and in 1969 his prime minister, General Lon Nol, demanded a Vietnamese withdrawal from its Cambodian bases and prohibited future Vietnamese use of the port of Sihanoukville as an entrepôt for the shipment of provisions to be used in South Vietnam.[33] In early 1970 Sihanouk went to Paris, reportedly in hopes of obtaining French support to persuade Hanoi to evacuate its bases in Cambodia. In his absence, Lon Nol staged a coup, deposing Sihanouk as chief of state. The new regime immediately renewed Lon Nol's earlier demand for the withdrawal of all Vietnamese revolutionary forces from Cambodian territory.[34]

Nguyen Van Nhat, p. 52.

[32] Interview with Mr. Kong Korn, deputy foreign minister of the People's Republic of Kampuchea, Ministry of Foreign Affairs, Phnom Penh, December 18, 1985. According to Kong Korn, China instigated the revolt. Hanoi agrees. See *The Truth,* p. 40. Curiously, Sihanouk echoed this claim at the time, asserting that Beijing was punishing Cambodia for pursuing better relations with the United States. He also accused Hanoi of supporting the insurgency. China was then in the throes of the Cultural Revolution, and was certainly unhappy with Sihanouk for his increasingly pro-Western stance, but it is questionable whether Chinese leaders at that time had sufficient motive to promote the uprising. For a similar comment, see Armstrong, pp. 207–208.

[33] Henry Kissinger, *White House Years* (Boston: Little, Brown, and Co., 1979), pp. 250–251.

[34] According to *The Truth,* p. 40, the KCP echoed this demand. Also see Prince Norodom Sihanouk, *War and Hope: The Case for Cambodia* (New York: Pantheon, 1980), pp. 7–8; and CKC, p. 128.

The coup presented Hanoi with both challenge and opportunity. It represented a distraction from the main battlefield in South Vietnam and complicated Hanoi's plans to launch a new offensive there. Lon Nol had made it clear to local representatives of the NLF that he would not budge from his demand that all Vietnamese forces evacuate Cambodia. On the other hand, the new government lacked the popular base that had sustained the government of Norodom Sihanouk, and was vulnerable to an insurrection. Hanoi may have decided very quickly that the problem could best be resolved by extending the war into Cambodia and supporting a revolt by anti–Lon Nol elements there. This plan had the added advantage of providing Hanoi with a rationale for a stronger Vietnamese presence in Cambodia and a greater role in shaping the political future of the country.[35]

For Hanoi's plan to work, several conditions were necessary. First, the strains in the relationship between the DRV and the KCP would have to be smoothed over to permit a coordinated effort against the common enemy. During the late 1960s DRV leaders had observed with disapproval the policies adopted by the new leadership of the KCP. The Pol Pot faction not only displayed a disconcerting tendency to suspect Vietnamese intentions in Cambodia, it also had ignored the principle of proletarian internationalism by adopting a strategy that posed a serious threat to the future success of the insurgency movement in South Vietnam. To make it worse, there was some evidence that Pol Pot himself admired the Cultural Revolution in China, arousing suspicion in Hanoi that he was little more than a tool of Beijing.

Second, the charismatic Sihanouk would have to be persuaded to serve as the titular head of the anti–Lon Nol movement to provide the internal popular support and the legitimacy on the global scene that only he could provide. Hanoi may also have viewed Sihanouk as a useful means of obtaining leverage over the obstreperous and vocally anti-Vietnamese Pol Pot. Finally, the plan would have to obtain the support or at least the benign approval of China. Although Vietnamese leaders may have already developed a lively suspicion of Chinese motives in Cambodia, Beijing's potential opposition to an escalation of the

---

[35] Henry Kissinger claims that Le Duc Tho made it clear to him that Hanoi intended to overthrow the Lon Nol government and replace it with one more acceptable to the North Vietnamese. See *White House Years,* p. 468.

revolutionary struggle there could be fatal to the success of the movement.[36]

From the outset, the task of reaching an accommodation with the KCP ran into snags. Within the Pol Pot leadership, suspicion of the Vietnamese ran deep, and it was only with difficulty that an arrangement was ultimately worked out. To provide the KCP with experienced cadres (and undoubtedly to strengthen Vietnamese influence over the movement), several thousand ethnic Khmer who had served with the Vietminh in the early 1950s but had been residing in North Vietnam since the end of the Geneva Conference were infiltrated into Cambodia to serve with the movement.[37]

According to Hanoi's version of the events, shortly after Sihanouk's arrival in China following the coup, DRV prime minister Pham Van Dong visited Beijing to persuade Sihanouk to serve as head of a new anti–Lon Nol united front in Cambodia and to induce the PRC to lend its support to the project.[38] At first, Sihanouk was reportedly undecided whether to agree to Hanoi's proposal. He had little liking for Pol Pot, and the feeling was undoubtedly mutual, since the latter had been tortured in Sihanouk's prison. Moreover, an agreement by Sihanouk to serve as head of a new Cambodian popular front would place him under the control of the North Vietnamese, a position he almost certainly did not relish. As an inducement, Pham Van

---

[36] Vo Dong Giang, Vietnamese deputy foreign minister, recently asserted that Hanoi did not initially suspect that Pol Pot was an agent of Beijing. Indeed, Giang believes that the Khmer Rouge leader was only gradually driven into the arms of the Chinese as a means of realizing his "big personal ambitions." As for the PRC, according to Vo Dong Giang, Pol Pot was only one of a number of potential "cards" that it could play to achieve its objectives in Indochina. Others were Lon Nol and Sihanouk himself. Interview with Vo Dong Giang, Ministry of Foreign Affairs, Hanoi, December 14, 1985.

[37] It is generally believed that Hanoi favored the idea, to strengthen their influence over the Khmer Rouge. Sihanouk, however, claims that Khieu Samphan, one of Pol Pot's lieutenants, informed him that it was done at the KCP's request. See *War and Hope,* p. 15. Gareth Porter, in "Vietnamese Policy and the Indochina Crisis," in David W.P. Elliott, ed., *The Third Indochina Conflict* (Boulder, Colo.: Westview Press, 1980), p. 92, says that they were sent to Cambodia at the KCP's request. Vietnamese sources in Hanoi imply that the decision was mutual. One PRK official said privately that he believed that most were sent at Hanoi's request. In any case, they soon became a source of serious discord between the two parties.

[38] *The Truth,* pp. 50–51.

Dong promised that after the victory of the coalition the DRV would provide explicit guarantees of Cambodia's independence and territorial integrity. To guarantee that eventuality, Sihanouk reportedly demanded China's blessing as a condition of his accepting the position.[39]

Chinese leaders reacted with extreme caution to the events in Cambodia. In the first place, the coup had taken place at a difficult time, when Beijing was beginning to reassess its relations with the Soviet Union and the United States. The Nixon administration had made a number of significant peace gestures to the PRC after coming to office in early 1969, and moderates within the party leadership wanted to pursue the possibilities of a rapprochement with the United States to curb the growing threat from Moscow. Other elements in Beijing, however, probably viewed the coup in Cambodia as evidence of the continued danger represented by U.S. imperialism. The internal debate over the implications of the coup undoubtedly made it difficult for China to adapt quickly to the situation in Indochina.[40]

Chinese leaders may also have suspected the motives of the North Vietnamese in promoting the formation of the new front, which could provide Hanoi with a vehicle to establish its dominance over Cambodia. Whatever the reasons, Chinese leaders were slow to react to the situation, and Hanoi's contention that Beijing considered an arrangement with the Lon Nol government may be correct. Chinese leaders accorded Sihanouk a warm welcome in Beijing, but gave no indication of their future actions. During the weeks following the coup, the Chinese ambassador remained in Phnom Penh, while the Cambodian ambassador to China, who had switched allegiance to Lon Nol, was allowed to remain in Beijing. According to Lon Nol, China offered to accord diplomatic recognition to his government provided that he permitted continued North Vietnamese use of the sanctuaries and the shipment of weapons to the insurgent forces there. Only when Lon Nol refused these conditions did the PRC decide to switch its support to the new front, which assumed the name of the National United Front for Kampuchea (FUNK).[41]

---

39 Jay Taylor, pp. 151–152; *War and Hope*, p. 39.

40 This internal power struggle has been described in Armstrong, p. 99, and John W. Garver, *China's Decision for Rapprochement with the United States, 1968–1971* (Boulder, Colo.: Westview Press, 1982), pp. 130–131.

41 Lawson, pp. 197–199. China's view of the sanctuaries is a matter of

Having secured China's promise of support, Sihanouk now sought to guarantee that Beijing would play a critical role in the organization by persuading the PRC to sponsor a conference attended by representatives of the revolutionary parties or governments in all three Indochinese countries. The Indochinese Summit Conference convened on April 24 in Gwangzhou. Sihanouk chaired the meeting, a decision that was taken not merely for symbolic reasons, since both Beijing and Hanoi needed his presence. Sihanouk attempted to use the position to his advantage and, with Chinese backing, to prevent Vietnamese domination over the new organization. He insisted on maintaining the separate identity of the revolutionary movements in Laos, Cambodia, and South Vietnam, and appealed to each to remain in its own territory unless it received permission from the others. But Hanoi refused his demand for the creation of a permanent organization to coordinate activities, asserting that it had no intention of allowing outside interference in planning operations. On balance, however, the conference had given Sihanouk some breathing room and had provided China with the opportunity to play at least an avuncular role as sponsor of the alliance. Beijing's role at the conference did not go unnoticed by Hanoi, which later charged that China had attempted to use the conference to promote its efforts to dominate the Indochinese countries.[42]

After the conference the new coalition of forces, involving supporters of Sihanouk, the guerrilla forces of the KCP (popularly known as the Khmer Rouge), and Khmer communists infiltrated from the DRV, began to build up the movement inside Cambodia. The border incursion by U.S. and South Vietnamese armed forces had disrupted Vietnamese base camps in the eastern provinces, but the revolutionary forces rapidly recouped their position and began to expand the area under their control. From the outset, however, problems were encountered in coordinating activities within the movement. Khmer resentment of Vietnamese advisers created an undercurrent of ethnic tension within the movement. The Pol Pot leadership of the

---

dispute. Hanoi claims that Beijing supported Phnom Penh's demand for the removal of Vietnamese liberation forces from the area. See *The Truth,* p. 40. Also cf. Seymour M. Hersh, *The Price of Power: Kissinger in the Nixon White House* (New York: Summit Books, 1983), p. 201.

[42] *The Truth,* p. 52; CKC, p. 127. For sources on the conference, see Jay Taylor, pp. 155–156, and Lawson, pp. 197–199.

KCP was intensely suspicious of the pro-Hanoi elements infiltrated from the DRV, and began to purge such "impure elements" from the party.[43]

China and the End of the Vietnam War

Relations between China and the DRV continued to deteriorate during the final years of the war. The negotiations at Paris coincided with the gradual improvement in Sino-American relations that culminated with President Nixon's visit to the PRC in 1972. In one respect, the rapprochement between Beijing and Washington operated to the benefit of the North Vietnamese. By demonstrating the trend toward moderation in Chinese foreign policy, it reduced Washington's fear of the possible consequences of a Communist victory in Indochina and made the Nixon administration more wiling to consider a compromise settlement of the war. To the Vietnamese, however, improving relations between Washington and Beijing served primarily to assure U.S. policy makers that they could attempt to intimidate Hanoi without fearing reprisals from China.

According to one student of Chinese foreign policy, the first clear sign of the shift in China's policy came in July 1971 when the PRC, for the first time since 1965, officially endorsed a DRV peace plan to end the Vietnam War. Previously, China had opposed negotiations and had urged the Vietnamese to continue their protracted war. Hanoi could not have been unhappy at Beijing's support of its proposal. But the announcement was followed shortly by the announcement of President Nixon's visit to China the following year. For Hanoi, the message of the Nixon trip was clear: China and the United States were preparing to force the DRV to agree to a compromise settlement of the conflict that would, as in 1954, betray the interests of the Vietnamese. Official statements emanating from Hanoi suggested that the North Vietnamese would not let themselves be bullied by larger powers.[44]

---

[43] Sihanouk says that Khieu Samphan told him that most would not "listen to reason" and had to be liquidated. See *War and Hope*, p. 15. For comments and sources on Khmer resentment of the Vietnamese, see my *The Communist Road*, p. 287.

[44] Jay Taylor, pp. 173-175; Lawson, pp. 212-214.

Chinese leaders were not ready to concede that their budding relationship with the United States had to lead to abandoning their long-term relationship with Vietnam, and they attempted to reassure the North Vietnamese of the constancy of their support for the victory of the Vietnamese revolution. But Hanoi was now increasingly convinced of Beijing's perfidy and was particularly incensed when President Nixon's visit to Beijing was scheduled in February, just before the launching of the North Vietnamese Easter offensive, which party leaders hoped would set the stage for a negotiated settlement on their terms. The DRV reacted to the Nixon trip with undisguised bitterness. One high official in Hanoi remarked that "while Nixon gets his 21 gun salute in Peking, we'll be giving him a different kind of salute in South Vietnam. There will be more than 21 guns. And they won't be firing blanks."[45]

It is not certain whether the policy shift in Beijing played a role in the decision by the North Vietnamese regime to accept the settlement that was eventually signed in January 1973, but there seems little doubt of Hanoi's conviction that the new Sino-U.S. relationship had operated to the detriment of their own revolutionary strategy. In early March, U.S. Secretary of State Henry Kissinger reportedly told a group of journalists that the administration now only needed to keep an eye on Moscow and knock out Vietnam. Although there was probably bitterness in Hanoi that both China and the Soviet Union were willing to sacrifice the needs of the DRV to satisfy their own interest in better relations with the United States, China's betrayal must have been particularly hard to swallow since it provided additional evidence of Beijing's long-term intentions in Southeast Asia; it led one high-level Vietnamese official to remark recently that the Nixon visit was viewed as a "stab in the back" in Hanoi and a turning point in Sino-Vietnamese relations. Far from desiring the withdrawal of U.S. military power from the region, Chinese leaders now appeared to encourage the United States to remain in the area as a counterforce to Soviet power in the region. As for the situation in South Vietnam, the PRC appeared to believe that the continued existence of two Vietnams was in its own national interest. In talks with Le Duan and Pham Van

---

[45] The quote is from the *New York Times,* February 20, 1972, cited in Lawson, p. 241.

Dong in June 1973, Chinese leaders advised their guests to refrain from renewing hostilities in the South for several years. In the words of Mao Zedong, as China's broom was not yet long enough to sweep the Chiang Kai-shek regime out of Taiwan, so Hanoi's broom could not yet sweep the revolution to power in South Vietnam. The PRC promised to maintain its assistance program to the DRV, but aid shipments were slow, and Hanoi later charged that aid stopped arriving entirely after 1973.[46]

Sino-Vietnamese rivalry also intensified in Cambodia, where the civil war had continued unabated after the Paris Agreement. At first, China was apparently dubious about the potential of the Khmer Rouge to seize power on their own and advised the latter to refrain from active efforts to overthrow the Lon Nol regime, while attempting to strengthen Sihanouk's position in the movement. By spring of 1974, however, Chinese leaders apparently had a change of heart and began to provide increasing aid to the Khmer Rouge. Pol Pot was invited to Beijing, where he met Chinese leaders and signed an aid agreement. China's action may have been prompted by evidence that Hanoi was attempting to strengthen its own hand in Cambodia, despite efforts by the Pol Pot leadership to purge pro-Vietnamese elements from the KCP. According to reports, the DRV may have considered an effort to remove Pol Pot from power, but eventually decided against it and settled for increasing the presence of Vietnamese forces in Cambodia. Two divisions of Vietnamese troops allegedly took part in the final offensive that seized Phnom Penh in mid-April of 1975.[47]

The tension in Sino-Vietnamese relations began to spill over into other areas as the long war gradually came to an end. In December 1973 the DRV, now beginning to turn its attention to postwar economic reconstruction, informed China that it intended to prospect for oil in the Tonkin Gulf and proposed nego-

---

[46] Lawson, pp. 230–244; Jay Taylor, p. 380; *The Truth,* pp. 54–56. The comment about China's "stab in the back" was made by Politburo member Le Duc Tho. See his interview in *Vietnam Courier* (June 1985), pp. 12–13.

[47] See Lawson, p. 282, and *Chinese Aggression Against Vietnam: Dossier* (Hanoi, 1979), p. 56. Sources in Hanoi now state openly that the Khmer Rouge could not have seized power in Phnom Penh without Vietnamese assistance. According to Deputy Foreign Minister Vo Dong Giang, the Khmer Rouge did not even possess the capacity to fire their own mortars. Interview with Vo Dong Giang, Ministry of Foreign Affairs, Hanoi, December 14, 1985.

tiations to settle potential disagreements over territorial rights. In mid-January the PRC agreed to talks. But acceptance coincided with the Chinese seizure of several islands in the Paracels that for several years had been occupied by the Saigon regime, a coincidence of timing that must have aroused suspicion in Hanoi. The first round of negotiations took place at the vice foreign ministers level in August 1975.

The negotiations soon ran into problems. The Vietnamese delegation suggested that the offshore boundary established by the 1887 convention should be accepted as the basis for determining the boundary of the mutual territorial seas in the gulf. The Chinese side rejected this proposal, pointing out that a division of the territorial waters in the gulf could not have been the original intent of the Sino-French agreement and that acceptance of the Vietnamese claim would give Hanoi two-thirds of the total area of the gulf. With the delegations unable to reach an agreement, the talks were suspended in November. The two sides agreed that no prospecting should take place in the rectangular area between the 18th and 20th parallels and the 107th and 108th meridians, the area under dispute. But the abortive talks had obviously caused irritation in the two capitals, and armed clashes began to occur along the common border. China proposed negotiations to settle the issue in March 1975, but Hanoi, pleading preoccupation with other issues, suggested that the issue be resolved by local authorities on the two sides.[48]

Conclusion

By 1975, then, Beijing and Hanoi were on a collision course, although the depth of the mutual antagonism was unknown to the outside world. As this chapter has shown, a number of factors were involved in the deterioration of relations, including several that promised to prove troublesome during the postwar period. But the main source of discord stemmed from the conduct of the Vietnam War itself and the different perceptions in the two capitals over the priority of the war in the broader context of global politics. Vietnamese leaders had apparently become convinced that China's Vietnam policy was rooted in a desire to maintain the division of Vietnam in order to facilitate postwar domination of Southeast Asia. The Chinese

---

[48] *The Truth*, p. 58.

were undoubtedly worried at Hanoi's growing dependence upon the Soviet Union and exasperated by the DRV's alleged lack of gratitude for a generation of Chinese assistance. It is not the intention here to evaluate the justice of such views. What is certain is that one source of the problem lay in the growing gap in the way leaders of the two regimes interpreted the significance of the dynamic forces at work on the world scene and how those forces affected the foreign policy goals of each state. Hanoi's world-view was locked into the Leninist vision of a bipolar struggle between the forces of world reaction and socialism. That vision, of course, coincided with the regime's need for Soviet support in its struggle against the United States. China, on the other hand, had become convinced that the costs of Soviet support were too high, and now inhabited a much more complex world characterized by national rivalries and the hegemonistic designs of the two superpowers. In the final years of the war, these divergent views led to increasingly strained relations between the two countries and increased the potential for postwar rivalry in the region.

IV

Descent into Conflict

As the long Vietnam War drew to a close, the once close relationship between China and the DRV was clearly entering into a period of rising tension. It is doubtful that either Hanoi or Beijing deliberately wished to provoke a breakdown in relations between the two countries. The DRV was faced with the intimidating challenges of economic reconstruction, political reunification, and the difficult transition to socialism; and Vietnamese leaders undoubtedly hoped for a period of peace in foreign affairs so that they could devote their time to domestic concerns. In China the party leadership was similarly preoccupied with internal issues, particularly the succession crisis between radicals and moderates connected with the impending deaths of Zhou Enlai and Mao Zedong.

But if neither China nor the DRV had an interest in exacerbating the situation, neither was evidently prepared to make a serious effort to seek a compromise on outstanding issues and prevent a further deterioration of relations. This obstinate attitude was amply demonstrated in meetings held between Vietnamese and Chinese officials during the summer and fall of 1975. In August a North Vietnamese delegation led by economic expert Le Thanh Nghi visited Beijing for preliminary talks on an economic trade and aid agreement for the postwar period. The visit attracted relatively little press coverage in the two countries, but was evidently marked by acrimony. Press reports indicated that Chinese officials were unhappy at the lack of gratitude and pro-Soviet attitude displayed by the Vietnamese.[1]

It soon became clear that there was much truth behind the reports. In September VWP general secretary Le Duan led an

---

[1] The *New York Times*, August 14, 1975.

official delegation to Beijing to discuss the aid pact. At the conference, disagreement surfaced over a number of issues. In the global arena, the two sides disagreed categorically over the current world situation. Vietnamese leaders refused to subscribe to China's new "Three Worlds" theory, which held that as the result of the emergence of Soviet "social imperialism" the socialist camp was no longer in existence. In China's view the USSR and the United States, as superpowers, composed the so-called First World. The developed countries made up the Second World, and the Third World, of which China was a part, was composed of the developing countries of Asia, Africa, and Latin America. Because the DRV refused to include a reference to "hegemonism" (a code word for Soviet expansionism), no joint communique was issued.[2]

China would later claim that differences over global problems did not affect the discussion of other issues at the conference, but it seems likely that Chinese irritation over Vietnamese intransigence may have influenced negotiations over an economic aid agreement. Deng Xiaoping allegedly informed Le Duan that, with the war over, China needed a "breathing space" and could no longer provide large amounts of technical assistance to Vietnam. At the end of the visit, the two sides announced agreement on a series of interest-free loans to the DRV and the signing of a protocol on an exchange of goods in 1976. But there would be no increase in Chinese aid, to the evident disappointment of the Vietnamese.[3]

---

[2] The theory of the "Three Worlds" was first enunciated by Deng Xiaoping in a speech before the U.N. General Assembly in April 1974. It was published by *People's Daily* on April 19, 1974. For an English language version, see King C. Chen, ed., *China and the Three Worlds: A Foreign Policy Reader* (White Plains, N.Y.: M.E. Sharpe, 1979), pp. 85–98. According to one Chinese source, Deng informed Le Duan at the conference that the two sides could disagree about the USSR without affecting other aspects of their relationship. See *Guoji wenti yanjiu* [Studies in international problems], no. 2 (October 1981), "The Truth about Sino-Vietnamese Relations," trans. in JPRS 79,661.

[3] Chinese leaders were evidently exasperated at Hanoi's tendency to accept assistance without feeling any sense of obligation in return. In March 1975 Mao Zedong's wife Jiang Qing (Chiang Ch'ing) quoted her husband as remarking: "Vietnam is a temple occupied by four chief monks who become master of anyone who gives them food and clothing." See Lawson, p. 239, citing *Background of China* (New York: China Information Service, June 12, 1975).

Le Duan's visit to Moscow in October stood in striking contrast to the strained atmosphere in Beijing. After apparently cordial talks, Vietnamese and Soviet leaders issued a joint communique announcing that Hanoi and Moscow had "identical views" on foreign issues. They also reached agreement for the unprecedented coordination of national economic plans for 1976 to 1980 and an aid package providing for Soviet assistance on more than 400 projects. Later reports suggested that Moscow had wanted an even closer relationship, perhaps suggesting that the DRV join the Soviet-sponsored Council for Mutual Economic Assistance (CMEA). The Vietnamese, probably hoping to obtain assistance from a variety of sources, including the advanced capitalist countries, demurred. But the meeting ended with the DRV and the USSR on increasingly intimate terms, and Hanoi had served notice to Beijing that it would not be bullied.

Focus on Cambodia

For the Vietnamese, the rising tension with China was not the only disquieting element on the international scene. The keystone of Vietnamese foreign policy in the postwar era was to be the "special relationship" (Hanoi's new version of the Indochinese Federation) with the new revolutionary governments in Laos and Cambodia, both of which had come to power in 1975. That relationship was quickly formalized with Laos. Laos immediately indicated that it would follow the lead of its mentor in limiting Chinese influence on Indochina, demanding the removal of 30,000 Chinese troops who had originally been sent to Laos to build roads in the northern provinces. In the meantime, several thousand Vietnamese troops remained in the country.[4]

Hanoi immediately encountered problems, however, with the new Pol Pot government in Phnom Penh. The first sign of difficulty came only a few days after the end of the war, when clashes broke out on the mutual border and on several disputed

---

[4] The Chinese road-building project had begun during the mid-1960s and had taken place with the tacit acquiescence of the neutralist government of Prime Minister Souvanna Phouma, who was reluctant to offend the PRC. For their removal, see Lawson, p. 281, and Taylor, pp. 162–163. Also see Gareth Porter, "Vietnamese Policy and the Indochina Crisis," in David W. P. Elliott, ed., *The Third Indochina Conflict* (Boulder, Colo.: Westview Press, 1981), p. 79. Laos later charged that China had not complied with its request to remove its personnel. See the *New York Times,* March 16, 1977.

islands in the Gulf of Thailand. The border conflict concealed a more significant source of dispute, the determination of the Pol Pot regime to reject Hanoi's "special relationship," which it viewed as a mere figleaf for the extension of Vietnamese domination over all of Indochina. At first, Hanoi appeared to view the Cambodian issue as a relatively minor irritation that could be resolved without recourse to violence. Shortly after the first border clashes, Le Duan visited Phnom Penh and offered to seek a negotiated solution to the territorial dispute. As for the "special relationship," according to a Chinese report Le Duan assured Pol Pot that it was premature to talk about such an arrangement and that Hanoi had no intention of seeking to impose its will on Cambodia.[5]

In actuality, while Vietnamese leaders were probably willing to compromise on the border issue, on the matter of the "special relationship" their views were considerably less flexible. As one Vietnamese official remarked to the French journalist R. P. Paringaux: "Naturally, we insist on special relations because we shared everything during the war." There was more than the memory of shared revolutionary experience in the Vietnamese attitude. While the Phnom Penh regime did not itself represent a serious threat to the security of the Vietnamese state—which became a single, unified Socialist Republic of Vietnam (SRV) in July 1976—behind the irritating figure of Pol Pot lay the greater menace posed by China. Beijing's behavior during the last years of the war had aroused suspicions in Hanoi that Chinese leaders were determined to use Cambodia—with its strategic position on Vietnam's vulnerable western frontier—as an instrument to resist the spread of Vietnamese influence in mainland Southeast Asia and perhaps to pressure the SRV to adopt policies more consistent with Chinese national objectives. To party leaders in Hanoi, then, the "special relationship" with Cambodia was not a negotiable issue but a matter of national survival.

---

[5] See Geng Biao (Keng Piao), "Report on the Situation on the Indochinese Peninsula," as reported in *Chung-kung yen-chiu* [Studies on Chinese communism], vol. 14, no. 10 (October 15, 1980), trans. in JPRS 77,074. Available evidence suggests that the border clashes were initiated by the Pol Pot regime. There have been unconfirmed reports, however, that they had been provoked, in part, by Vietnamese refusal to withdraw its troops from disputed areas along the frontier.

Vietnamese fears of Chinese involvement with the Pol Pot regime were at least partly justified. By mid-1974 Beijing had probably concluded that the Khmer Rouge represented China's best chance to maintain its influence in Cambodia and had begun to provide the movement with increased military assistance. According to a document cited by the SRV and allegedly seized after the Vietnamese occupation of Phnom Penh in January 1979, Pol Pot made a secret trip to Beijing in May 1975, a few weeks after the end of the war. At that meeting, China reportedly agreed to provide the new regime with economic assistance and to send a mission to Phnom Penh to train the Cambodian armed forces and provide technical assistance to the new administration. In return, Pol Pot indicated his support for Beijing's "Three Worlds" theory and took China's side in its dispute with the Soviet Union.[6]

Yet Chinese leaders must have felt uncomfortable with their new ally. Pol Pot's behavior since his accession to power in Cambodia did not inspire confidence among the moderate elements now controlling Chinese foreign policy. Phnom Penh's radical policies and its brutal purge of all suspected class enemies (including thousands of urban residents of Chinese origin) had caused great unrest within the country, and specifically within the party and the armed forces, where Sihanoukists and pro-Hanoi elements had been singled out for extermination. Pol Pot compounded the problem by ignoring the suggestion of his Chinese advisers to use Prince Sihanouk as a charismatic symbol of the new regime, which now styled itself Democratic Kampuchea. Altogether, Pol Pot must have seemed an unreliable tool with which to confront the tough and experienced Vietnamese. Chinese leaders therefore initially sought to defuse the crisis in an effort to prevent a direct confrontation between Hanoi and Phnom Penh which could only redound to the disadvantage to the latter, and to its patron in Beijing. While the PRC may have attempted to apply diplomatic pressure on the SRV to evacuate its troops from Cambodia (many of whom had reportedly remained after the end of the war), it counselled caution to the

---

[6] See *The Chinese Rulers' Crimes Against Kampuchea* (Ministry of Foreign Affairs, People's Republic of Kampuchea, April 1984), pp. 76, 86. Also cf. Wilfred Burchett, *The China, Cambodia, Vietnam Triangle* (New York: Vanguard Books, 1979), pp. 165–168.

Pol Pot regime and advised it to seek a negotiated settlement of the territorial dispute dividing the two countries. But Beijing's efforts met with little success. The Pol Pot leadership continued to adopt a belligerent attitude toward Hanoi, which it accused of harboring a deep historical desire to destroy the Khmer people. By the end of 1977 the clashes on the border had intensified to the level of open warfare, and much of the army and the party organization was in open revolt.[7]

Chinese leaders were caught in a vise over Cambodia. Although fearful that the erratic behavior of Pol Pot could embroil China in a direct confrontation with Vietnam, they could hardly acquiesce in what they perceived to be Hanoi's plan to achieve total domination over all of Indochina. Their policy toward Cambodia throughout 1977 reflected that ambiguity. In a secret speech on foreign policy, Foreign Minister Huang Hua indicated that China's Cambodian policy was based on four points: (1) that the three Indochinese states should establish a cease fire and seek a negotiated settlement on the basis of the principles of the 1970 summit; (2) that, if the Indochinese states so desired, China would be willing to serve as a mediator to restore mutual solidarity, friendship, and cooperation; (3) that China would not "take the side of any state" to aggravate tension or provide military aid that would aggravate tension; and (4) that China supported the stand of Cambodia against Soviet "social imperialism" and would act to protect Cambodian territorial integrity and national sovereignty by giving all possible assistance.[8]

---

[7] The most graphic indication of Khmer Rouge resentment of the Vietnamese is contained in *Black Paper: Facts and Evidences of the Acts of Aggression and Annexation of Vietnam against Kampuchea* (Democratic Kampuchea: Ministry of Foreign Affairs, 1978). For indications of China's displeasure with the policies of the Pol Pot regime and its effort to restore Sihanouk to power in Phnom Penh, see Geng Biao's secret speech, cited in n. 5. Geng says that 4,000 pro-Hanoi members of the armed forces were killed or imprisoned. Earlier, Zhou Enlai had vainly advised Khieu Samphan to avoid following the example of China's Great Leap Forward, and of the need for a gradual advance to socialism. *War and Hope,* p. 86.

[8] See the secret speech by Huang Hua, translated in Chen, *China and the Three Worlds,* p. 272. It is interesting to note that Huang's speech put the primary blame for the troubles in Indochina not on the SRV but on Soviet "social imperialism," suggesting that Chinese leaders had not yet abandoned hope that Hanoi would see reason and back away from its growing ties with Moscow. In his speech, Huang reported that China had informed Vo Nguyen Giap of the Chinese proverb "Don't chase away the wolves from the front door only to admit

Until mid-1977, then, both Hanoi and Beijing had held back from a direct confrontation over Cambodia. The Vietnamese, despite their growing irritation with the truculent attitude adopted by the Pol Pot regime, refrained from openly aggressive actions to replace it with a leadership more amenable to their plans for Indochina. The PRC, while openly maneuvering to maintain the independence of the Phnom Penh regime, attempted to avert a crisis and appeared reluctant to make a formal commitment to its obstreperous client.

During the last half of the year, however, the dispute began to intensify. The primary cause appeared to be the behavior of the Pol Pot regime itself. Perhaps emboldened by a new military aid agreement negotiated in Beijing in September, Pol Pot may have felt he had total backing from China. During the fall months, the level of fighting along the border increased, and the Phnom Penh regime stubbornly refused a compromise solution.[9]

In November a Vietnamese delegation led by Le Duan visited Beijing for talks with Chinese leaders on the Cambodian dispute. The Vietnamese may not have entirely abandoned the hope that the PRC was not irrevocably committed to the Pol Pot regime; they reportedly requested the Chinese to apply pressure on Phnom Penh to seek a settlement of the crisis. Chinese leaders, however, may have concluded that Hanoi was intent upon realizing its intention to force Cambodia into an Indochinese Federation and therefore refused to pressure the Pol Pot regime into a settlement. To the contrary, they demanded a total withdrawal of Vietnamese troops from eastern Cambodia.[10]

The failure to reach an understanding with Beijing and the continued obstinacy of the Pol Pot regime had begun to exhaust Hanoi's patience. At the same time, the rising level of discontent within Cambodia suggested the possibility of a different solution to the problem. During the fall of 1977 Hanoi began to establish contacts with rebel leaders inside Cambodia to discuss coordinated efforts to promote an uprising that would overthrow the Pol

---

tigers and leopards through the back door." China must have patience with the Vietnamese, Huang concluded. They would eventually learn the costs of allying with Moscow.

[9] For a source sympathetic to Hanoi's claim that captured documents reveal that the Pol Pot regime felt it had Chinese support for offensive strategy toward the Vietnamese, see Burchett, p. 170.

[10] See Geng Biao's secret report (n. 5).

Pot regime and replace it with a government amenable to better relations between the two countries. The prime instrument to bring about this plan was So Phim, a regional commander of the Pol Pot regime who had become so disenchanted with the confrontational policies that he apparently felt could only lead Cambodia to disaster.

Whether Hanoi had now committed itself to an overthrow of Pol Pot is not clear. On the diplomatic front, it continued to press for a negotiated settlement. In January, Prime Minister Pham Van Dong issued an appeal to "fraternal countries" (presumably China) to help resolve the crisis, and Vice Foreign Minister Phan Hien went to Beijing in mid-month to resume talks with Cambodian leaders.[11] But Beijing had now apparently discarded the diplomatic option, and in December the CCP Central Committee had met to consider an increase in the level of economic and military assistance to the Phnom Penh regime. According to one source, the main subject of debate may have been the level of Chinese commitment. Some party leaders apparently recommended the dispatch of Chinese warships to the Gulf of Thailand, or possibly even of Chinese troops to Cambodia to demonstrate the seriousness of China's commitment. In the end, however, the committee decided to take no action that could lead to a direct Chinese military involvement in the conflict, restricting itself to an agreement to increase the shipment of arms and other military equipment to Cambodia. In mid-January, Beijing sent Zhou Enlai's widow Deng Yingzhao (Teng Ying-chao) on an official visit to Phnom Penh. One clear purpose of the visit was to symbolize China's support for the regime. But Deng may also have carried with her Beijing's advice to pursue more moderate policies and a threat to cut off aid if such advice was ignored.[12]

In early February, Hanoi submitted a new proposal for a settlement of the growing dispute with Phnom Penh. But the recent abortive talks with Beijing in November and the signs of

---

[11] The *New York Times,* January 18, 1978.

[12] Deng's message sparked an angry retort from Phnom Penh. See Stephen P. Heder, "The Kampuchean-Vietnamese Conflict," in Elliott, *The Third Indochina Conflict,* pp. 45–46. For information on the aid program, see *Far Eastern Economic Review* (*FEER*), March 17, 1978, p. 10, and April 21, 1978, p. 19. China's reasons for avoiding direct military intervention are contained in Geng Biao, "Report," pp. 10–11.

growing Chinese support for Democratic Kampuchea in succeeding weeks had probably already convinced Vietnamese leaders that the stiff position taken by the latter had firm Chinese backing. With private negotiations with dissident elements in Cambodia showing signs of success, Hanoi decided to turn to the military option.

In January, Radio Hanoi had openly called for the overthrow of the Phnom Penh regime. In mid-February, the party Central Committee held its fourth plenum. The meeting took place at a moment of crisis for the Hanoi regime. Abroad, the events of the previous few weeks appeared to confirm the fears of party leaders that China was firmly committed to support of the Pol Pot regime. At home, difficulties stemming from the difficult transition to a peacetime economy had created widespread alienation among the populace and in some areas—notably among recalcitrant minority groups in the South—open dissidence against the socialist system. The growing crisis imposed serious strains on the party leadership. At the Fourth National Congress of the VWP in December 1976 (at which time the party had changed its name to the Vietnamese Communist party, or VCP) a number of top members, including Politburo member and ex-ambassador to China Hoang Van Hoan, had been dismissed from their positions because of their presumed opposition to the growing pro-Soviet orientation of Vietnamese policy. Doubts over the wisdom of the regime's hardline policy toward China persisted, however, and it is likely that they were raised at the February plenum. Tension had also begun to build up over internal policy. Ideologues claimed that the nation's economic and social problems could only be solved by a rapid transition to socialism, while moderates counseled a temporary retreat to stimulate economic growth and dampen social unrest.[13]

To make matters worse, some saw a direct connection between the regime's external and internal problems. A major source of the regime's economic difficulties stemmed from the activities of the overseas Chinese community in Saigon (now renamed Ho Chi Minh City), whose manipulation of the market had created instability in the distribution and circulation of goods. Chinese agents had reportedly been active in the overseas

---

[13] For a discussion of the intraparty dissension over policy, see my *Vietnam Since the Fall of Saigon* (Athens: Ohio University Press, 1985), chap. 2.

Chinese community since the mid-1960s, when radical elements formed youth groups and shock brigades to study Mao Zedong Thought. After 1975, according to Vietnamese sources, such activities were resumed, as the radical elements attempted to subvert the loyalty of ethnic Chinese in the SRV and create problems for the Vietnamese economy. Chinese agents were also operating in the tribal areas along the Sino-Vietnamese border, where distrust of the lowland Vietnamese was strong, and in an apparently preemptive measure to avert the danger of open revolt, the Hanoi regime placed two of the most prominent military officers of tribal minority origin, generals Chu Van Tan and Le Quang Ba, under house arrest.[14]

The deterioration in Sino-Vietnamese relations also affected the resolution of the territorial dispute between the two countries. By the mid-1970s, evidence of potentially significant oil reserves in the South China Sea made ownership over the Paracels and the Spratlys a matter of considerable economic importance. The DRV had taken no action in response to the Chinese seizure of islands in the Paracel chain in January 1974. Shortly after the end of the war, however, units of the Vietnamese People's Army seized six islands in the Spratlys that had previously been under South Vietnamese administration and issued a map labeling all of the islands Vietnamese territory. During Le Duan's visit to Beijing in September, Deng Xiaoping reportedly raised the issue and offered to open negotiations, but Hanoi refused. During the next two years there were no talks over the border issue, and clashes periodically erupted over the common frontier. Then, in 1977, the Vietnamese newspaper *Quan Doi Nhan Dan* (People's army) published a map marking both the Spratlys and the Paracels as Vietnamese territory.

China reacted to the claim with outrage, contending that Pham Van Dong's letter to Zhou Enlai in 1958 had served as formal Vietnamese recognition of Chinese sovereignty over both island groups. As further evidence it cited the fact that geographical atlases published in the DRV had called the islands by their Chinese names and had explicitly labeled them as Chinese. Hanoi retorted that Pham Van Dong's 1958 letter to Zhou had not specifically recognized Chinese ownership of the islands. To the contrary, Hanoi asserted that "the spirit and letter" of the

---

[14] The arrests were reported in *FEER,* August 10, 1979.

note "were confined to recognition of China's twelve-mile territorial waters."[15] During a short visit to Beijing in April 1977, Prime Minister Pham Van Dong suggested talks about the Paracels, but China declined. Talks on the land border and the ownership of the Tonkin Gulf had also proved abortive. By 1978 no settlement of the territorial was in sight, and border clashes began to increase.

To distrustful minds in Hanoi, then, the pattern of events since the end of the Vietnam War strongly suggested that the Beijing regime was attempting to lock the SRV in a vise and force Vietnam to bend to its will. Statements by high officials compared Cambodia to "a dagger pointed at the heart of Vietnam." To the veteran leadership in Hanoi, bitter experience confirmed that only a determined attitude and an offensive strategy could enable the Vietnamese people to confront and vanquish their enemies. Thus at the Fourth Plenum meeting in February 1978, the party adopted a tough policy on both the foreign and domestic fronts to resolve the crisis.

The rationale for action in Cambodia was clear. Evidence was accumulating that Pol Pot was firmly in Beijing's camp and that the latter would attempt to manipulate the situation in Cambodia to realize its own foreign policy objectives in Southeast Asia. If Hanoi hoped to prevent China from stabilizing its position in Phnom Penh, it must act soon. An open invasion by Vietnamese troops would be the most decisive solution, but it

---

[15] See the statements by the SRV Ministry of Foreign Affairs in *Vietnam News Bulletin*, "Memorandum on Chinese Provocations and Territorial Encroachments upon Vietnamese Territory," April 10, 1979, and "White Book on Vietnamese Archipelagoes," reported in VNA, September 28, 1979, and translated in FBIS, volume 4, October 1, 1979. This source contains documentary evidence supporting Vietnamese claims to the islands. Beijing's version was reported in *Beijing Review*, March 30 and August 24, 1979. According to the former, Pham Van Dong admitted that Hanoi had implied its recognition of Chinese sovereignty in 1958 to avoid a dispute that might lead Beijing to reduce the level of aid to the DRV. China released documents supporting its claim in "China's Indisputable Sovereignty over the Xisha and Nansha Islands," *Beijing Review*, February 18, 1980. References to the abortive talks in September 1975 are in *Beijing Review*, May 25, 1979, and in "White Book on Vietnamese Archipelagoes." In his secret speech in 1977, Foreign Minister Huang Hua remarked that China would not take any immediate action to recover the Spratlys. He noted that when the time was right, China would confiscate them; thus there would be no need for negotiations.

could cause serious international repercussions and possibly provoke a direct confrontation with China. A general uprising led by anti-Pol Pot rebels in Cambodia and supported discreetly by the SRV was less risky and certainly less costly, but success would be less certain. In the end, the plenum decided to proceed with plans to provoke an internal uprising led by So Phim while keeping in reserve an alternative plan to topple the Phnom Penh regime through direct intervention.

The party moved with equal dispatch to resolve the internal crisis. Despite the opposition of moderates, the plenum approved a proposal to move rapidly to end the power of the overseas Chinese in the South. In mid-March, Hanoi suddenly announced the nationalization of all private enterprises above the family level. While the move affected the entire commercial and manufacturing sector, the primary target was the large and still economically powerful overseas Chinese community in Ho Chi Minh City. After the end of the war in 1975, the revolutionary regime had seized the property of a few wealthy Chinese traders and industrialists, and a few were placed on trial for economic "crimes against the people." In general, however, the private sector had been left untouched as the regime attempted to promote economic recovery and stimulate industrial growth after the long and destructive war. Now, under the impact of twin difficulties in domestic and foreign affairs, the regime shifted course.

The Refugee Crisis

The impact of Hanoi's new strategy on regional tensions was immediate, and massive. During the spring, thousands of refugees began to cross the land border into China. The first to leave were ethnic Chinese from the North. Many complained that in the weeks preceding their flight they had been subjected to harassment because of their racial origins. Others fled as a result of rumors that they would be dismissed because of impending war with China or because they had been fired from their jobs or forced to accept Vietnamese citizenship.[16] Many complained after they reached their destinations that Vietnamese officials had connived at their departure and forced them to pay extravagant sums to leave.

---

[16] For a detailed account of refugee complaints, see Bruce Grant, *The Boat People: An "Age" Investigation* (Harmondsworth: Penguin, 1979).

Hanoi's move took place at a time when official attitudes in Beijing had already been inflamed as a result of the Cambodian crisis. Chinese leaders were almost certainly aware of the decisions that had been taken at the February plenum in Hanoi. Hanoi's decision to seek the overthrow of the Pol Pot regime struck directly at the heart of Chinese foreign policy objectives in Indochina. Its decision to nationalize industry and commerce also represented no less a direct challenge to Beijing. In China's eyes, the move was clearly directed against the overseas Chinese in the South; and while Beijing had encouraged ethnic Chinese living in Vietnam as well as elsewhere in the region to adopt local citizenship, it continued to show periodic solicitude for the welfare of Chinese living abroad, leading many governments in the area to suspect that the overseas Chinese were viewed in the PRC as a tool of Chinese foreign policy.

Beijing reacted quickly to the exodus of refugees from Vietnam, citing refugee accounts claiming persecution and charging that Hanoi was trying to drive all ethnic Chinese out of the country. The chairman of the Overseas Chinese Commission in Beijing lodged a strong protest against official mistreatment of the overseas Chinese, while the Ministry of Foreign Affairs charged that Hanoi had reneged on the 1955 agreement calling for gradual assimilation. To back up its protests, China announced the cancellation of a number of aid projects underway in the SRV. Indeed, a number of outside observers have noted that the refugee crisis marked a significant stage in the escalation of the Sino-Vietnamese dispute and that, beginning in late May, the level of Chinese press criticism of the SRV began rapidly to intensify.[17]

Hanoi responded in kind, asserting that its policy was not racially motivated and that it was only attempting to do what all previous Communist regimes, including the PRC itself, had already achieved—to complete the transformation of private commerce and industry. The SRV charged additionally that much of the unrest among the local Chinese had been deliberately incited by the PRC, whose embassy in Hanoi was actively fomenting suspicion and disorder by spreading fallacious rumors among the overseas Chinese community.[18]

---

[17] *Washington Post,* May 27, 1978.
[18] Ibid., May 30, 1978. For further evidence, see Burchett, p. 181, and Paul Quinn-Judge, "The Vietnam-China Split: Old Ties Remain," *Indochina Issues,*

Where does the truth lie among these charges and counter-charges? On the one hand, the evidence concerning the motives for Hanoi's action is ambiguous. Beijing's assertion that Hanoi from the start deliberately attempted to drive the ethnic Chinese out of Vietnam is not substantiated by the available evidence. To the contrary, there are indications that refugee departures were initially discouraged and that illegal flight was severely punished. On the other hand, there is considerable evidence that the decision to nationalize private industry and commerce was motivated, in good measure, by a desire on the part of the Hanoi regime to "resolve the overseas Chinese question." Whether or not refugee reports that the party leadership had established a special bureau to deal with the "Chinese question" are valid, it is clear from statements appearing in the official press as the crisis evolved that the regime felt that it had good reason to suspect the loyalty of the local Chinese community and that Beijing was using it as a tool in its foreign policy. Comments by refugees of Chinese extraction confirm Hanoi's suspicion that many ethnic Chinese did indeed indicate their primary loyalty to China as the crisis evolved. Whatever the original intentions of the Hanoi regime, then, as the crisis developed, Vietnamese leaders became increasingly convinced that the overseas Chinese community represented not only an undigestible foreign body in the socialist society of the SRV, but also a potential threat to its national security. Once that conclusion was reached, the regime began to encourage the departure of all those ethnic Chinese who desired to leave and began to remove them from the administration and the party itself.[19]

Was Hanoi justified in its charge that Beijing consciously fostered the problem? There is some evidence that pro-Chinese elements were active in promoting the rumor that the Vietnamese government, in case of war with China, would treat ethnic Chinese as potential traitors, and a number of refugee accounts indicate that some groups were actively encouraged to emigrate to China. To the degree that this was true, it is likely

---

no. 53 (January 1985), p. 4.

[19] According to one report, all ethnic Chinese have now been removed from the VCP. See Quinn-Judge, "The Vietnam-China Split," p. 4. For statements indicating that many Chinese gave their loyalty to China, see Grant, pp. 94–96, 104.

that Beijing was implicated. That does not affect the fact, however, that many overseas Chinese were leaving because of concrete grievances over the treatment that they were receiving at the hands of the government.

During the late spring and summer of 1978, the war of words between Beijing and Hanoi rapidly escalated into a major crisis. In early June, Hanoi approved a Chinese request to send ships to pick up potential refugees at ports designated by the SRV. But problems soon developed. The PRC requested permission to open a consulate in Ho Chi Minh city to process applications for emigration, but Hanoi refused. A deadlock also developed on procedures for the landing of the ships, so they were forced to remain offshore and eventually left without permission to dock at Vietnamese ports. Finally, high-level talks opened at China's request in early August. In the meantime, the flood of refugees crossing the land border into China had increased rapidly, surpassing 140,000 by July, when the PRC tightened controls on the border, accusing Hanoi of sending spies and other "bad elements" to sabotage the Chinese effort to relocate the refugees. The talks themselves opened with bitter words on each side and soon adjourned without result.

The accelerating crisis now began to exert repercussions on the very structure of the relationship between the two countries. Tension along the mutual border increased amidst reports of a troop buildup on both sides of the frontier. In late June, Hanoi announced its intention of joining CMEA, stating that the decision had been necessitated by the cutoff in Chinese assistance. A few days later, Beijing announced that all its remaining aid projects in the SRV had been terminated and all Chinese personnel instructed to return to China. Hanoi accused China of applying "crude and blatant pressure" on Vietnam.

The Vietnamese Invasion of Cambodia

At the February plenum, the Vietnamese party leadership had approved a proposal to remove the Pol Pot regime by an internal uprising. The key to the success of this strategy lay in the emergence of a resistance movement strong enough to challenge the Pol Pot regime for power. But in May, Pol Pot's forces attacked rebel headquarters, and So Phim was captured and executed. In the meantime, there were signs of strengthening ties between Phnom Penh and Beijing. In early June, Deng Xiaoping met with Foreign Minister Ieng Sary and declared that China would adopt tougher measures if Vietnam continued to pressure the Phnom Penh regime. In July, Pol Pot's minister of defense Son Sen visited Beijing and obtained a promise of increased military aid.[20]

In mid-summer the VCP Central Committee convened its Fifth Plenum in Hanoi. With plans for a general uprising thwarted by the death of So Phim, and growing indications of Chinese involvement in the Cambodian crisis, the party leadership approved a new plan to launch an outright invasion of Cambodia to overthrow the Pol Pot regime. Rebel forces in Cambodia would take part in the attack and provide a cloak of legitimacy for the operation, but the brunt of the attack would be borne by Vietnamese regular forces. The decision was fraught with risks, not only because of the danger of provoking a counterreaction by China, but also because it would complicate Vietnamese relations with Western nations and also necessitate an understanding with Moscow. But party leaders must have felt a sense of urgency to resolve the problem before Beijing could consolidate its position in Phnom Penh. The decision was undoubtedly a controversial one. A few days after the conference adjourned, *Nhan Dan* criticized party members who showed weakness in facing the crisis and warned that the party must "leave behind and discard weak elements incapable of enduring trials or bent on giving up or betraying the cause."[21]

Once the decision had been made, Hanoi's most pressing need was to seek the support of Moscow. Soviet assistance would be critical, not only to provide military equipment for the invasion but, even more important, to serve as a deterrent against a possible Chinese counterattack. Vietnamese leaders had undoubtedly consulted with the Soviet Union earlier and may have raised the issue of increased military assistance and a

---

[20] See *The Chinese Rulers' Crimes against Kampuchea* (PRK: Ministry of Foreign Affairs, April 1984), p. 99. Geng Biao's "Report" indicates that by December, China would have provided Democratic Kampuchea with enough equipment for three divisions, and food, medicine, and ammunition for 100,000 troops. See p. 13.

[21] *Nhan Dan,* August 4, 1978. According to one source, some Central Committee members recommended a softer line toward China so that Hanoi could concentrate its attention on the domestic crisis. See "A hint of purges yet to come," *FEER,* September 1, 1978, p. 9.

possible treaty of alliance and cooperation. Soviet leaders had suggested such a treaty a few years previously, but the Vietnamese had demurred in order to retain maximum flexibility in their foreign policy. In the current situation, however, Hanoi could not afford such luxury, and it is probable that party leaders now asked the Central Committee to assent to a treaty, even though it would commit Hanoi irrevocably to a policy of dependence on the USSR and take Sino-Vietnamese relations another step down the fateful road to a final break.

The decision could not have been an easy one for Moscow, since it would set back Soviet plans to improve relations with China. Moreover, it would undoubtedly complicate Soviet relations with other nations in Southeast Asia and possibly with the United States. On the other hand, it would give Soviet leaders greater leverage over the Vietnamese and a potentially valuable strategic position in Southeast Asia that could be used against either Beijing or Washington. It is likely that Moscow demanded increased military rights in Vietnam as a quid pro quo for its assent to a treaty.

For Hanoi, one of the potential drawbacks to a treaty with the Soviet Union was the impact that it could have on Vietnamese relations with the non-Communist world. It was probably for this reason that the SRV requested a delay in the signing of the treaty in order to provide an opportunity to seek better relations with the ASEAN countries and the United States. During the summer months Pham Van Dong embarked on an extended tour through Southeast Asia to discuss economic cooperation and a possible nonaggression treaty. In September the SRV dropped its conditions for the establishment of diplomatic relations with the United States.

Neither ploy worked. The ASEAN countries, suspicious of Hanoi's motives, did not respond to Pham Van Dong's initiative, while the United States, now committed to normalization of relations with China and increasingly inclined to view Vietnam as a member of the Soviet bloc, declined to pursue Hanoi's offer. After several weeks in New York City waiting for a response from the Carter administration, Deputy Foreign Minister Nguyen Co Thach left for Moscow to sign the treaty. Some observers have criticized the failure of the Carter administration to respond to Hanoi's overtures, arguing that Washington's hostility forced Hanoi into the arms of the Soviet Union. This is a debatable point. I am inclined to believe that Hanoi was committed to its treaty with Moscow regardless of the state of U.S.-Vietnamese relations. In any case, given the delicate state of Sino-American negotiations over the restoration of diplomatic relations, Washington was in no position to provide Hanoi with guarantees against a Chinese attack.

According to current Deputy Foreign Minister Vo Dong Giang, the decision to sign a treaty of alliance with Moscow was made in mid-summer as a result of the growing threat from China. Hanoi also hoped to improve relations with other Great Powers, including the United States, in order to isolate Beijing, but the decision to sign the treaty with Moscow was not related to the course of U.S.-Vietnamese relations. The public announcement of the treaty did not take place until November, said Giang, for "technical reasons."[22]

During the autumn of 1978, Hanoi prepared for its invasion of Cambodia, scheduled for the beginning of the dry season in December. Vietnamese armed forces in South Vietnam were beefed up, while units of the PAVN strengthened their position in Cambodian territory. Intelligence sources reported an increase in military equipment sent by airlift from the USSR. The political scene was not neglected. In early December, anti-Pol Pot rebels announced the formation of a new Kampuchean National United Front for National Salvation (KNUFNS) under the leadership of an ex-commander of Khmer Rouge forces named Heng Samrin.

The signing of the Soviet-Vietnamese treaty in early November and Hanoi's obvious preparations for an invasion of Cambodia presented China with a strong challenge. During the summer and fall months, China increased the level of its military assistance to the Phnom Penh regime. There were an estimated 6,000 Chinese military advisers in Cambodia, and a somewhat larger number of technicians. Beijing began to escalate the propaganda war against Hanoi, promising the Pol Pot regime "resolute support" and warning Vietnam that its aggressive behavior

---

[22] Interview with Vo Dong Giang, December 14, 1985. For comments critical of U.S. foreign policy at the time, see Derek Davies, "Carter's Neglect, Moscow's Victory," *FEER,* February 2, 1979, and Robert G. Sutter, "China's Strategy toward Vietnam and Its Implications for the United States," in David W. P. Elliott, *The Third Indochina Conflict,* pp. 186–188.

would not go unpunished. And Deng Xiaoping embarked on a tour of Southeast Asian capitals to build up support for an anti-Vietnamese coalition among the ASEAN states.[23] Yet there was little in the way of concrete action to back up Beijing's strong words. Although intelligence sources reported a buildup of Chinese forces on the Vietnamese border, there were no obvious signs of war preparations. And in October, Deng Xiaoping publicly announced that China would not send troops into Cambodia. When Pol Pot visited the PRC the following month, Chinese leaders reportedly advised him to use the strategy of protracted war to counter aggressive actions by the Vietnamese.[24]

The crisis in Cambodia presented China with its most excruciating foreign policy dilemma of the post-Vietnam War period. Hanoi's uncompromising stance on the Indochina issue and its obvious preparations for an invasion of Democratic Kampuchea represented a direct affront to China and to its overall foreign policy objectives in Southeast Asia. But given the self-imposed constraints on Chinese military involvement established by the Central Committee the previous December, its options were limited. Lacking a common border with Cambodia, China could only assist its ally by airlift or by sea, for both of which the PRC lacked adequate logistical capability. Active Chinese intervention in case of a Vietnamese invasion would be costly and would impose severe limitations on the program of domestic modernization that the Deng Xiaoping leadership hoped would result in rapid economic growth in the 1980s.

The issue of how to deal with the Vietnamese challenge was probably dealt with at a series of leadership meetings that culminated in the holding of the Third CCP Plenum in mid-December 1978. The plenum took place at a moment of vigorous debate within the party leadership over domestic as well as foreign policy issues. Domestic issues centered on Deng Xioaping's program for rapid modernization and the campaign to rid the party of radical elements connected with the Gang of

---

[23] Deng had only moderate success in rounding up support in ASEAN capitals, where the residual resentment against Chinese arrogance and Beijing's past support for local revolutionary movements still inspired resentment.

[24] This advice was reportedly repeated by a Chinese delegation that visited Phnom Penh later the same month. See "Pol Pot eyes the jungle again," *FEER*, December 15, 1978, p. 34.

Four and put a definitive end to the Maoist era in China. In the foreign policy arena, the crisis in Indochina was certainly a major issue, but as always, China's major concern was its relations with the global powers. For Beijing the "Vietnam problem" was only part of its larger concern over how to deal with the Soviet threat. The Cambodian crisis was also affected by China's rapidly evolving relationship with the United States. The Third Plenum had been preceded only a few days by the December 15 announcement that remaining obstacles to a normalization of relations had been removed. Any decision to launch a military operation against Vietnam would pose the risk both of worsening Sino-Soviet relations and impeding the establishment of diplomatic relations with the United States.

The debate over how to deal with the situation in Cambodia, then, was unavoidably entangled in the debate over other domestic and international issues facing the Chinese leadership. Although relatively little information is available on the course of the discussion, the debate probably focused, as during the crisis of 1965, on the source of the threat, its seriousness, and how to respond.[25] There was probably little disagreement over the fact that Vietnamese actions in Indochina posed a serious challenge to Chinese foreign policy objectives in Southeast Asia. There may have been serious disagreement, however, over the source of the threat and how to respond. To some, Vietnamese aggressiveness was simply the most visible manifestation of a Soviet effort to encircle China. As such it was a direct challenge to Beijing, and called for a strong reaction. To others, the Cambodian crisis may have appeared to be a simple product of Vietnamese expansionism, and as such was not directly related to the Sino-Soviet power struggle. In this view, the main threat to China was in the north, where several hundred thousand Soviet troops were posted on the Chinese border. As for the growing Soviet military presence in Vietnam, it was in actuality directed more against the United States and its strategic position in Southeast Asia than against the PRC.

Such disagreements inevitably affected the debate over how to respond to the crisis. Some undoubtedly argued that for rea-

---

[25] For speculation on the debate, see Sutter, pp. 180–186, and Gurtov and Hoang, *China under Threat,* chap. 6.

sons of prestige or of precedent China was obligated to make a strong response to Hanoi's challenge. Otherwise, Hanoi (and Moscow) would become convinced that China, divided over policy and preoccupied with internal problems, was unable to act decisively in foreign affairs. Others may have retorted that a Chinese attack would simply play into the hands of the enemy, since it would delay the program of economic modernization and create obstacles to better relations with the United States. Equally important, it would drive the Vietnamese deeper into dependency on the Soviet Union.

Whether a definitive decision was reached at the Third Plenum or after the Vietnamese invasion of Cambodia on December 25 is not known. Chinese leaders had laid the groundwork for intervention before the meeting, when a Chinese note to the SRV on December 13 declared that there were limits to China's forbearance and restraint and warning Hanoi that if it persisted in its course, it "must be responsible for the consequences."[26] In any event, it is clear that after mid-December, China began to prepare actively for war. On December 24 the official press quoted Mao's well-known phrase uttered years before in a warning to the United States: China will not attack. But if China is attacked, it will certainly counterattack.

If the Chinese had intended such statements as a deterrence to the Vietnamese, they were not successful. On Christmas Day Vietnam launched a general offensive at several points along the Vietnam-Cambodia border. The attack, labeled a "war of liberation," involved the active participation of anti–Pol Pot guerrilla forces, but the brunt of the assault was borne by 100,000 regular forces of the PAVN.[27] The Khmer Rouge defenders fought bitterly, but they were outnumbered, short on firepower, and unprepared for the ferocity and the direction of the attack. In early January the Pol Pot regime abandoned the capital and retreated to a redoubt in the Cardamom Mountains. At the same time, a new People's Republic of Kampuchea (PRK) headed by Heng Samrin was announced in Phnom Penh. A week later the

---

[26] The *New York Times,* December 13, 1978.

[27] According to Truong Chinh, currently SRV Chief of State, Vietnamese forces responded to Khmer Rouge attacks and crossed the border in self-defense. Then, rebel Khmer forces launched a general offensive and uprising. See Truong Chinh, *On Kampuchea* (Hanoi: Foreign Language Press, 1980), p. 19.

new regime concluded a treaty of friendship and cooperation with the SRV.

The Sino-Vietnamese War

China did not immediately respond to the Vietnamese invasion. It is doubtful that the attack had taken the Chinese leadership by surprise, although the rapidity of Phnom Penh's collapse had probably not been anticipated. But Beijing appeared to be in no hurry to administer its "lesson" to Vietnam. One probable reason for the delay was to take advantage of the trip by Vice-Premier Deng Xiaoping to the United States, scheduled for late January.[28] To Chinese leaders, the opening to Washington was important, above all, as a means of countering the Soviet threat and ending China's long isolation on the international scene. But the new relationship with the United States could also serve as a centerpiece in Beijing's strategy to isolate Hanoi and discourage the USSR from undertaking military action in response to a Chinese attack on Vietnam. From mid-1978 the Carter administration had quietly cooperated with China in attempting to counter Vietnamese actions in Cambodia. The refugee crisis and the announcement of the Soviet-Vietnamese treaty attracted critical comment in Washington and gave the Carter administration additional reasons to act in concert with the PRC.[29] Chinese leaders undoubtedly hoped that the Carter administration would be sympathetic to China's plan to punish Vietnam. If not, Deng's visit would at least represent visible proof of the importance of the new relationship and give the impression that China's policy had Washington's blessing.

The United States was aware of the Chinese buildup through intelligence sources, and U.S. policy makers, while not lacking in sympathy for China's desire to punish Vietnam, were clearly concerned at the impact of a possible Chinese attack on U.S. policy objectives elsewhere. Carter administration officials especially feared that Deng would take advantage of his visit to give the impression of U.S. support for China's action and cause

---

[28] Geng Biao claims that one reason for the delay in launching the attack was to prepare public opinion for war. See his "Report," p. 16. See p. 5 for his comment on describing Beijing's surprise at the rapidity of the collapse of the Khmer Rouge.

[29] For China's plan to enlist U.S. aid, see ibid., p. 13.

further damage to the deteriorating U.S.-Soviet relationship. That concern became a reality in late January when Deng, in Washington, publicly stated that China might take action against Vietnam. "If you don't teach them some necessary lessons," he warned, "it just won't do."[30]

Such words undoubtedly caused acute discomfort in the White House. But the Carter administration was reluctant to take any step that could set back the normalization process; and although President Carter and other high U.S. officials advised against an attack in their private talks with Deng, Washington did not make a public statement to that effect until after Deng's departure. Washington had unwillingly become an accomplice of Chinese foreign policy objectives in Southeast Asia.[31]

On February 17, Chinese troops crossed the border at several points on the Vietnamese frontier. According to Western intelligence sources, China had two armies in the border areas, backed up by eight divisions of local forces. There were a reported 1,000 planes in the region, including fifteen squadrons of fighters. Many, however, were outdated MiG-17s and MiG-19s. To match this armada, Vietnam had a total of 600,000 combat troops; but the cream of the PAVN was operating in Cambodia, and only about 60,000 to 80,000 troops were near the Chinese frontier, supported by the local forces and the militia. The Vietnamese, however, were better armed, and their air force included 120 new MiG-23s and a few MiG-25s and U.S. F-5s.[32]

According to Deng Xiaoping, the Chinese attack force comprised about 100,000 troops, with additional units of 120,000 kept in reserve. Virtually from the outset, it was clear that the invasion was not an all-out assault with the intent of overrunning the Red River Delta and seizing Hanoi. Not only were the number of troops involved in the initial attack too small to penetrate far beyond Vietnam's border defenses, but statements by Chinese officials themselves suggested that the Chinese attack would be limited. On February 20, Deng confirmed the limited nature of the attack, and a few days later

---

[30] The *New York Times,* January 31, 1979.

[31] For two first-hand accounts, see Jimmy Carter, *Keeping Faith* (New York: Bantam, 1982), pp. 204–209, and Cyrus Vance, *Hard Choices: Critical Years in America's Foreign Policy* (New York: Simon and Schuster, 1983), pp. 120–121.

[32] The *New York Times,* February 21, 1979.

Beijing announced that China had no intention of entering the Red River Valley or seizing Hanoi. The purpose of the war was to punish Vietnam for its aggressive attitude and demonstrate that there were limits to Chinese tolerance.[33]

During the first days of the war, Chinese troops advanced with relatively little opposition, seizing the border towns of Lao Cai and Dong Dang and advancing about ten miles into Vietnamese territory. With its main force units outnumbered two to one in the battle area, Hanoi chose not to involve its regular forces in combat, and the brunt of the resistance was borne by regional and paramilitary units backed by three regional border divisions. Neither side made extensive use of its air force. Hanoi did not move reinforcements from Cambodia but did place three PAVN divisions in a defensive position around Hanoi, from Yen Bay on the Red River to Quang Yen on the coast.

Beijing's assurances that Chinese troops would not enter the Red River Delta and threaten Hanoi were undoubtedly intended, above all, for the ears of the Soviet leaders in Moscow. The Soviet Union had reacted cautiously to the invasion. Moscow demanded an immediate withdrawal of Chinese forces and promised to stand by its treaty commitment, which called for mutual consultation but not an automatic involvement in case of an attack on either party. But it carefully avoided provocative actions. Reserve leaves for Soviet troops on the Sino-Soviet border were canceled, but there was no announcement of mobilization and no evidence of substantial troop movements in the border region. The Soviet Union did start an air lift to Vietnam and sent a flagship cruiser of the Sverdlov class to the South China Sea. Privately, however, Soviet officials told foreign diplomats their belief that the war would be limited and expressed confidence in the ability of the Vietnamese to handle their own defenses.

On February 22, after a short pause to regroup, Chinese forces resumed their advance through mountain passes along the

---

[33] Ibid., and February 27, 1979. On February 19, Deng had remarked to the visiting secretary-general of the Organization of American States that the Chinese people had to "take a position to demonstrate that they do care" and could not seem to be indifferent and allow themselves to be pushed around. See the *New York Times,* February 21, 1979.

Sino-Vietnamese border. Their deepest penetration was in the west, at Lai Chau, where they penetrated within a few miles of the mountain base of Dien Bien Phu. But the major focus of Chinese attention was further to the east at Lang Son, the major Vietnamese city in the frontier region. Because Vietnamese resistance had been stiffer than Chinese strategists had anticipated, Beijing may have concluded that the occupation of Lang Son would provide symbolic proof of the success of the invasion and an excuse to break off the attack and begin withdrawal. The battle for Lang Son began in late February. More than 200,000 troops were involved in combat on both sides. China had seventeen divisions inside Vietnam or in the immediate vicinity, to face about 100,000 Vietnamese. Relying on infiltration by small units rather than mass attack, the Chinese gradually tightened their grip around Lang Son, and by early March the city was nearly encircled, with the attackers holding the high ground. Hanoi now recognized the importance of the battle for Lang Son and for the first time committed main force units to prevent its capture; but Chinese superior forces and artillery prevailed, and the city finally fell on March 4.

Official sources in Beijing described the capture of Lang Son as evidence of victory, but such statements could not hide the fact that the results of the invasion must have been a disappointment to Chinese leaders. Although Beijing had undoubtedly achieved some if its objectives—capturing twenty cities, causing considerable damage to Vietnamese defenses in the frontier area, and demonstrating its willingness to use military force to achieve its foreign policy objectives—the invasion had not compelled Hanoi to withdraw substantial numbers of its own forces from Cambodia, and the Chinese army, despite its superiority in numbers, did not achieve a smashing victory. Indeed, the Vietnamese had demonstrated to the world their ability to resist the Chinese assault without being forced to commit their own main force units. At the same time, the invasion had disclosed serious weaknesses in the Chinese armed forces. According to Western intelligence reports, the People's Liberation Army (PLA) showed poor coordination of air and artillery, a lack of modern equipment, and serious logistical problems.[34]

---

[34] For an analysis of the results of the war, see the articles by Drew Middleton in the late February and early March issues of the *New York Times*. Chinese officials would later concede privately that the results had been disastrous. See

In sum, the overall results of the invasion, from China's standpoint, were ambivalent at best. The assault had not forced the Vietnamese to reduce their pressure on the Khmer Rouge. As for teaching Hanoi a "lesson," the Vietnamese had not broken under the assault, and indeed were strengthening their border defenses to make the administration of a second lesson even more difficult. In the international arena, while many states in the vicinity publicly supported the PRC and privately commented that Hanoi had asked for it, the attack did arouse concern in some capitals that China had used force to punish a smaller neighbor, thus arousing old fears of Chinese domination over Southeast Asia.

With the fall of Lang Son, the focus of the conflict shifted to the opening of negotiations. Beijing first proposed peace talks on March 1. Hanoi rejected the proposal on the grounds that Chinese troops were still "trampling on our soil," but countered with a proposal of its own that talks could begin on condition that all Chinese troops first be withdrawn across the frontier. On the fifth, China reiterated its offer and announced the start of a pullout. On the fourteenth, the SRV agreed to begin negotiations after the completion of the Chinese withdrawal. After a brief diplomatic skirmish over Hanoi's claim that Chinese troops remained at several areas inside Vietnam, agreement was reached at the end of March; in mid-April a Chinese delegation arrived in Hanoi to begin peace talks.

It is doubtful that either side placed high expectations on the possibility of a negotiated settlement of the issues dividing the two countries. The fact is, neither Beijing nor Hanoi was in a mood to compromise. The sharp difference in perspective was clearly demonstrated in the peace plans presented by each side. China presented an eight-point proposal calling for discussion of all the issues dividing the two countries. Hanoi, claiming that the only issue was restoration of peace on the border, countered with a three-point proposal calling for a cease fire, establishment of a demilitarized zone along the border supervised by an international commission, and restoration of normal relations. The Chinese delegation retorted that no settlement could be achieved without a thorough review of all issues causing tension between the two countries. Lacking even an agreement on procedures for

---

the *New York Times,* January 5, 1980.

conducting negotiations, the talks became simply a forum for propaganda, and they were adjourned at China's request in March 1980.[35]

Conclusion

The Sino-Vietnamese conflict, and the events that led up to it, had a major impact on the structure of international politics in Asia. The war not only brought a definitive end to an alliance that had lasted for nearly half a century, it also led to a realignment of the regional power balance and threatened, for the first time in more than a decade, to bring the Great Powers to the brink of confrontation in Southeast Asia.

The origins of the conflict, and the nature of its impact on regional and international politics, has understandably aroused considerable debate in academic and foreign policy circles. It is clear that there were several factors involved in the breakdown in Sino-Vietnamese relations. It is more difficult to single out the underlying factor most responsible for the outbreak of armed conflict. Although it is generally assumed that the primary source of tension lay in the Cambodian dispute and the growing Soviet presence in Vietnam, some have suggested that the refugee issue may have been the precipitating factor, pointing out that Beijing began to escalate its direct criticism of Hanoi only after the beginning of the refugee exodus in mid-May of 1978.

The problem is partly one of semantics. There seems no doubt that Hanoi's treatment of the overseas Chinese community in Vietnam had caused severe irritation in Beijing and may have served to convince Chinese leaders that Vietnamese behavior had become intolerable and required a strong response from the PRC. If such is the case, the refugee issue may have been a precipitating factor propelling the Sino-Vietnamese dispute to its violent climax. It is unlikely, however, that Hanoi's treatment of its Chinese population was the primary cause for China's decision to go to war. On previous occasions China had tolerated severe mistreatment of Chinese nationals in various countries in the region without its precipitating a breakdown in relations. In this instance, other issues, notably the Cambodian dispute and the security concerns that surrounded it on both sides, had al-

---

[35] The *New York Times,* March 6, 1980. For the proposals submitted by the two sides, see *Beijing Review,* May 4, 1980, and VNA, April 18, 1979.

ready brought relations between China and Vietnam near the breaking point. In all probability, the refugee issue—which, whatever its symbolic importance, was still essentially a secondary concern to Chinese leaders—was used by Beijing as a signal to Hanoi of its anger over the course of Vietnamese policy and eventually as a pretext to justify an effort to punish Vietnam for its aggressive and stubborn behavior.

The underlying source of the dispute, then, must be sought in those issues that had brought Sino-Vietnamese relations to the brink of conflict in the first place. The dispute over Cambodia was obviously a central factor in the gradual breakdown in mutual relations, and may have been the single most important immediate cause of Beijing's decision to go to war. It is clear, however, that relations were already deteriorating before the Cambodian dispute came to a climax in 1978. Cambodia, then, is also at least partly an external manifestation of deeper concerns in Hanoi and Beijing. Some of these concerns had been instrumental in the deterioration of relations that took place in the final years of the Vietnam War.

These concerns were various on both sides. Beijing was angry at Hanoi's failure to take Chinese advice on how to conduct the struggle in the South and concerned that Vietnamese aggressiveness could involve the PRC in a direct confrontation with the United States. It was also irritated at the growing Vietnamese dependence upon the Soviet Union and on Hanoi's failure to take China's side in the Sino-Soviet dispute. For its part, Hanoi was infuriated at China's failure to offer adequate support for the Vietnamese struggle for national reunification and at Beijing's tendency to place its own national interests ahead of the broader concerns of the world revolution. In the eyes of Vietnamese leaders, China was guilty of following a policy of national aggrandizement rather than a Leninist one of proletarian internationalism. Hanoi was indignant at what it considered China's attempt to resume its former hegemonistic role in Southeast Asia and to restore in modern guise the tributary relationship with Vietnam that had been adopted by the imperial court in the precolonial period.[36] Finally, both sides were

---

[36] The Vietnamese conviction that China is striving to achieve a dominant position in Southeast Asia was expressed to me in considerable detail during a recent interview at the Institute of International Relations in Hanoi. According to a specialist in Sino-Vietnamese relations at the institute, Southeast Asia is a key

suspicious of the territorial claims that might be advanced in the future by the other.

It is clear from the above that there were multiple causes of the deterioration of Sino-Vietnamese relations that took place at the end of the Vietnam War. Some involved practical concerns related to national security, territorial integrity, and national independence. Others related to questions of ideology or other factors connected with the Cold War. Still others appeared to be a product of mutual suspicion and perceptions rooted in the distant past.

What, then, were the respectives roles of history and of contemporary factors related to the Great Powers' struggle in the conflict? Should the Cambodian dispute, and the Sino-Vietnamese war that followed it, be viewed as a revival of historic patterns of rivalry and suspicion that had temporarily been submerged by Western imperialism and the Cold War and now revived after the fall of Saigon? Or was the regional conflict in Southeast Asia in actuality a "proxy war" in which the local contestants were essentially surrogates in the global struggle between the Great Powers?[37]

The role of the Great Powers in the Indochina conflict is obvious. The Cold War served to transform what would otherwise have been a confrontation between local forces in the region into a global conflict intertwined with the Sino-Soviet dispute and the worldwide ideological struggle between the forces of socialism and capitalism. Once the prestige and the security concerns of the Great Powers became involved, the regional dispute was inexorably sucked into the vortex of the global Cold War. A similar process had taken place during the Franco-Vietminh conflict in the early 1950s, when an anticolonial struggle for na-

---

area in Chinese policy, today as during the traditional period. The constant goal of Chinese policy since 1949 has been to restore the dominant position in the area that had been lost during the colonial period. The focal points of Beijing's strategy in the region are Indochina and Indonesia (thus China's attempt to stage a coup with the Communist party of Indonesia in 1965), and the primary instrument of Chinese subversive efforts are the overseas Chinese and "Maoist" cliques within local Communist parties. Interview with Nguyen Phuong Vu, December 9, 1985.

[37] For a trenchant analysis of the historical forces at work in the region, see William S. Turley and Jeffrey Race, "The Third Indochina War," *Foreign Policy*, no. 38 (Spring 1980). The description of the conflict as a "proxy war" was made by U.S. national security adviser Zbigniew Brzezinski.

tional independence was transformed by the entry of China and the United States into an integral element in the Great Power conflict of the postwar era. With that transformation, the conflict could no longer be resolved on the basis of the reconciliation of local interests alone, but was irrevocably intertwined into the fabric of Great Power rivalry.

The importance of Cold War factors, however, should not be exaggerated. In the first place, there is no evidence that either Moscow or Washington played an active role in instigating the crisis. To the contrary, there are indications that both the Great Powers were somewhat reluctant to become actively involved in a dispute that could seriously jeopardize their other concerns in the region and perhaps risk a direct Soviet-U.S. confrontation. Both the United States and the Soviet Union were preoccupied with problems in other areas of the world, and not inclined to place a high priority on the situation in Indochina. Both undoubtedly viewed the evolving crisis in the region in the context of the broader Soviet-American relationship; and while both were anxious to protect their interests in the area, they acted in such a way as to limit their own involvement in order to reduce the likelihood of a direct confrontation over the issue. Moscow probably viewed the crisis as an opportunity to fill the vacuum left by the withdrawal of the United States from the region after the Paris Agreement of 1973, and the treaty with the SRV was carefully crafted to provide Moscow with a military presence in Vietnam without dragging the USSR into an open-ended commitment to defend Vietnamese interests in the area. Washington was even more circumspect, refraining from a posture of open support to China and implicitly criticizing Beijing's decision to resort to arms.

Great Power interests, then, were clearly implicated in the crisis, but they were not critical either in bringing it about or leading it to its final military confrontation. The real roots of the conflict must be sought in the complicated relationship between China and Vietnam and between Vietnam and Cambodia. Phnom Penh, Hanoi, and Beijing all based their actions on the conviction that their larger adversary was determined to reassert its past dominance over its weaker neighbor. In all cases, that conviction was based to a considerable degree on historical experience. The Pol Pot regime was almost irrational in its fear—as expressed in the famous *Black Book*—of Vietnam's historical determination to realize the total submission and even the cultural extinction of the Cambodian state. Hanoi, in turn, appeared convinced that the primary goal of Chinese foreign policy was to reassert its traditional political and cultural domination over Indochina. For its part, China charged that Hanoi's actions in Indochina were actually a mask for Soviet designs to achieve hegemony in Asia. There may have been an element of hyperbole in the charges. But the violence of the confrontation, and the rapidity with which it came about, cannot be explained without reference to the primordial fears that characterized the attitudes and the behavior displayed in each capital.

Were such suspicions justified? In the absence of additional information about the nature of policy objectives in Moscow, Beijing, and Hanoi, it is difficult to attempt a definitive answer to this question. Certainly all the nations in the region had legitimate security concerns that came under threat as the crisis unfolded. And there may be an element of truth in the fears expressed in all three capitals. From the perspective presented here, however, it is probable that all of the main actors in the crisis—Phnom Penh, Hanoi, and Beijing—may have exaggerated the threat to their own security. It is doubtful that either Hanoi or Beijing, or for that matter Moscow, were possessed by the single-minded determination to bludgeon their weaker neighbor into submission. In fact, all of the larger parties were motivated primarily by the desire to protect their own security interests by restoring their traditional role of benevolent patron over their smaller neighbor. All were initially reluctant to become directly involved in a direct confrontation over the issue and attempted to achieve their objectives without recourse to violence. But the sense of historical grievance and distrust made compromise more difficult and sped the dispute to its tragic conclusion.

Whatever the origins of the Sino-Vietnamese conflict, it represented a serious setback for the foreign policy objectives of both nations. In the case of China, it brought about the very result that Beijing's policy had been designed to prevent, the introduction of Soviet military forces on its vulnerable southern flank. For Vietnam, the results were more ambivalent. The occupation of Cambodia and the creation of the PRK put Vietnam within reach of its cherished goal of a "special relationship" among the three Indochinese countries. And, in the USSR, Hanoi now had a powerful protector. But the cost of national security was high. The primordial fear of generations of Vietnamese patriots—a hostile China on the northern frontier—was once again a grim reality.

V

The Struggle for Cambodia

Whatever the primary causes of the breakdown in Sino-Vietnamese relations, the main focus of tension between the two countries in the period following the 1979 invasion was directed at Cambodia. Although both Hanoi and Beijing had initially sought to avoid a confrontation over that unfortunate country, the course of events had negated such efforts and thrust it into the crux of the dispute.

In this struggle for predominance, the Vietnamese possessed a number of advantages. In the first place, as a contiguous state, Vietnam was in a strategically superior position to impose its influence over Cambodia. By contrast, China had no direct border with Cambodia and would be forced to supply the Khmer Rouge through Thailand. Second, Hanoi possessed the advantage of occupation. Vietnam had only to stabilize the situation in Cambodia and present the world with a fait accompli. With nearly 200,000 Vietnamese troops inside the country, China would be hard pressed to maintain a credible resistance movement against the new PRK. In addition, that task would be hindered by the internal brutality and unsavory international reputation of the overthrown Pol Pot regime.

China was not totally without advantages, but they were less tangible. Beijing undoubtedly hoped to capitalize on the widespread distaste for Vietnam's open invasion of Cambodia by mobilizing international support against recognition of the new pro-Hanoi regime. Chinese leaders could also make use of the anxiety over Vietnamese expansionism elsewhere in the region, particularly among the ASEAN countries. China might be able to exploit the internal vulnerability of Vietnamese society, now in a state of virtual crisis, to intimidate Hanoi into a settlement. And, of course, China could take advantage of its superior military power to threaten to administer a second "lesson" to its headstrong neighbor.

Consolidating Power in Phnom Penh

For Hanoi, the first task was to consolidate power in Cambodia. Initially, this was less a military than a political problem. The forces of the overthrown Pol Pot regime, now regrouping in the Cardamom Mountains and along the Thai border, did not pose an immediate military threat to the Vietnamese occupation troops in the country. Hanoi did face an intimidating challenge, however, in establishing the legitimacy of the new regime in Phnom Penh. The problem had both domestic and external implications. Domestically, it was partly a question of numbers. Most of the pro-Hanoi members of the KCP (now renamed, once again, the Kampuchean People's Revolutionary Party, or KPRP) had been purged during the reign of Pol Pot. Some knowledgeable observers estimated that there were only about a hundred party members as the PRK assumed power in January 1979. Most literate Cambodians had been executed or had fled the country during the Pol Pot years, and few remained to help rebuild society under its new stewardship.[1]

Beyond the problem of numbers was the issue of popular acceptance. While the bulk of the population probably accepted the new regime as a welcome change from the brutal behavior of the fanatical Khmer Rouge, the presence of nearly 200,000 Vietnamese occupation troops could not but give ordinary Khmer the impression that the Heng Samrin regime was nothing but a creature of Hanoi. To win local support, Hanoi tried to impose a new brand of communism, Vietnamese style. The cities were reopened and a measure of private commerce was resumed. The vast work camps set up by the Pol Pot regime in rural areas were dismantled and replaced by smaller "production solidarity teams" composed of several families from a common village. By means of such policies, Hanoi and its client regime in Phnom Penh attempted to alleviate the economic crisis that had brought production to a standstill and widespread hunger to much of the

---

[1] According to a Vietnamese source, between 1975 and 1979 the Pol Pot regime had executed four Central Committee members, 79 secretaries and members of the zonal party committees, and several hundred other party and government officials. PRK sources listed the number of professionals killed by the regime as 594 doctors and pharmacists, 675 college professors, 18,000 school teachers, 10,550 students, 191 journalists, and 1,120 government officials. See *The Chinese Rulers' Crimes against Kampuchea* (PRK: Ministry of Foreign Affairs, 1984), pp. 80–81.

population. The ruthless elimination of intellectuals was halted, and the practice of Buddhism and other forms of religion was permitted to resume.

The issue of legitimacy, of course, also had implications on the international scene. Hanoi had apparently not anticipated the hostile reaction to the Vietnamese invasion and was initially taken aback by foreign criticism of its action. In the months immediately following the invasion, however, Vietnam made little effort to deflect such criticism, in the apparent belief that it would be just a matter of time before the international outcry died down. When China and the ASEAN countries proposed an international conference under the aegis of the United Nations, Hanoi accused the sponsors of "brazenly meddling" in the internal affairs of Cambodia. The PRK, it said, was the sole legitimate representative of the Cambodian people, and the United Nations had no right to take the issue up as a matter of discussion.

By the end of the year, however, it had become clear that, outside the Soviet bloc, international support for its occupation of Cambodia was minimal, and Hanoi began to see the need for dialogue. In January 1980 a meeting of the foreign ministers of the Indochinese countries called for an "exchange of views" with other countries in Southeast Asia to set up a region of peace, neutrality, and stability. In the spring Vice Foreign Minister Nguyen Co Thach embarked on a tour of the region during which he attempted to drive a wedge between the PRC and ASEAN by insisting that Cambodia was a problem between China and Vietnam. As a gesture of Hanoi's peaceful intentions, he offered to sign a nonaggression pact with Thailand and suggested the establishment of a demilitarized zone between Thailand and Cambodia to reduce the likelihood of conflict between Thai and Vietnamese troops along the border. In the meantime, Hanoi sources began to hint that the PRK could be broadened to include new elements. But Hanoi would not budge on ASEAN's demand that Vietnamese troops be removed and that elections be held under international supervision to select a nonaligned government in Cambodia. At a conference held in July, the three Indochinese countries announced that socialism in Cambodia was "irreversible," and the "special relationship" an accomplished fact.

Forming a Coalition

If it was Hanoi's immediate task to stabilize the new regime in Cambodia, it was China's to prevent it. Because of the geopolitical features of the situation, Beijing's military options were limited. Chinese leaders were compelled to devise an approach that combined several components—political, military, economic, and diplomatic—into a comprehensive strategy to force Hanoi to abandon its plan to create a Vietnam-Laos-Cambodia alliance. The key to that strategy was the Khmer Rouge. Chinese leaders were well aware of the "shortcomings and mistakes" committed by the Pol Pot regime. But it was the only political force in Cambodia linked to China and strong enough to pose a credible threat to the new government in Phnom Penh. China's first priority, then, must be to burnish the image of the Pol Pot regime to make it more attractive on the domestic and international scene. Immediately following the fall of Phnom Penh, Chinese leaders held talks with Foreign Minister Ieng Sary in Beijing. At that time, Deng Xiaoping reportedly lectured his guest on the realities of the new situation and the importance of broadening the base of the movement. To provide a symbol that could appeal to a broad spectrum of opinion in Cambodia and win international support, Deng suggested that Prince Sihanouk, now living in asylum in China, be appointed Chief of State. He also advised the Khmer Rouge leader on the need to abandon the draconian policies of the past and to promulgate a new program based on such widely popular issues as democracy and patriotism. After Ieng Sary's departure, *People's Daily* publicly called for the creation of "an extensive national, democratic and patriotic united front" that focused, not on class struggle, but on the defense of the nation against Vietnamese aggression.[2]

Beijing's second problem was to round up international support for an anti-Hanoi movement in Cambodia. The Third CCP Plenum, in December 1978, had set the plan in motion by

---

[2] The *New York Times*, February 20, 1979. Information on Ieng Sary's meeting with Chinese leaders in January is contained in *Some Evidence of the Plots Hatched by the Beijing Expansionists and Hegemonists against the Kampuchean People* (PRK: Ministry of Foreign Affairs, 1982), p. 18. According to this source, Pol Pot was reluctant to make an approach to the "unsteady" Sihanouk, whose dislike of the Khmer Rouge was notorious; but Deng Xiaoping was insistent, arguing that "the fox is not as bad as the wolves."

calling for the establishment of an international united front centered on opposition to Soviet "socialist imperialism." One pillar of that front would rest on the new alliance with the United States. Another would be based on a new relationship to be forged with ASEAN, whose support would add credibility to China's proposed coalition of anti-Vietnamese forces to oppose the new regime in Cambodia. Forming such an alliance would not be a simple matter, not only because of the unsavory reputation of Pol Pot, but also because some members of ASEAN, notably Indonesia and Malaysia, were traditionally suspicious of China and viewed Vietnam as a potential bulwark against the threat of future Chinese expansion into the region.

For China, the most critical of the ASEAN states was Thailand. Because of the difficulty of supplying the Khmer Rouge by sea, China would require Thai permission to ship goods overland through Thailand. In early 1979 Beijing approached Thai leaders to request permission for the Khmer Rouge to use Thailand as a headquarters and to allow the shipment of war material to guerrilla forces operating inside Cambodia. As an inducement to Bangkok, China may have promised that the pro-Beijing Thai Communist party (TCP) would no longer seek the violent overthrow of the Thai government.[3]

Beijing was also prepared to make a number of concessions to obtain support from other ASEAN countries. Some of these concessions would not be easy, for they would reduce Chinese influence in Cambodia and undercut its credibility with Communist parties throughout Southeast Asia. China attempted to respond to some of ASEAN's concerns while refusing or temporizing on others. It persuaded Sihanouk—who at first had wanted to deal with the Vietnamese—to lend his support to the search for a coalition. It prevailed upon Pol Pot to step down as head of the Khmer Rouge, although he remained commander-in-chief of the armed forces. And it promised to support free elections leading to the creation of a parliamentary system of government in Cambodia, publicly declaring that conditions in that country

---

[3] See Geng Biao's "Report on the Situation in the Indochina Peninsula," pp. 11–12. According to PRK sources, Beijing had asked Bangkok for permission to use Thai air space to transport supplies into Cambodia as early as November 1978. See *The Chinese Rulers' Crimes*, p. 99. For a report detailing cooperative activities between the TCP and the Pol Pot regime, see *Journal of Contemporary Asia*, vol. 12, no. 4 (1982), pp. 501–516.

were not ripe for the imposition of a government based on Marxist-Leninist principles. To alleviate ASEAN fears of China's intentions in the region, Beijing promised not to support revolution in the region, although it refused to cut its ties to local Communist parties in the Southeast Asian countries.

During 1981 the anti-Hanoi coalition in Cambodia gradually began to take shape. After painstaking negotiations between the Khmer Rouge and two non-Communist factions loyal to Prince Sihanouk and Son Sann—a politician who had served under Sihanouk—differences were resolved, or at least papered over, and the coalition was formally created in June 1982. China promised to provide the new government, called the Coalition Government of Democratic Kampuchea (CGDK), with diplomatic and military support.[4]

A third goal of Beijing's Indochina strategy was to weaken Vietnam through political, economic, and military pressure. According to Western intelligence sources, China maintained at least 150,000 troops in South China to tie down Vietnamese defenses in the border area. Beijing attempted with some success to promote insurgent activities among tribal minorities in the Central Highlands, in the mountains near the Sino-Vietnamese frontier, and in northern Laos, where rebel tribesmen, some of whom had been trained in camps in South China, harassed the pro-Hanoi government in Vientiane.[5] China also attempted to increase its presence in the South China Sea, building up its fleet and strengthening its naval facilities on Hainan Island. While the PRC did not attempt to seize islands in the Spratlys occupied by the SRV, Chinese ships actively patrolled the area, and Beijing periodically reiterated its formal claim of ownership over the islands. In the Gulf of Tonkin, China ignored Vietnamese warnings and granted drilling rights to Western Oil companies west of the island of Hainan.[6]

---

[4] For the tortuous negotiations over the formation of the coalition, see Jacques Bekaert, "Kampuchea's 'Loose Coalition': A Shotgun Wedding," *Indochina Issues*, no. 22 (December 1981).

[5] For sources, see AFP, October 10, 1983, translated in FBIS, volume 4, October 11, 1983, which cites Hanoi's charge that China was raising a "traitors' army" among tribal groups and the overseas Chinese; and the *New York Times*, January 5, 1980. November 12, 1982, Chinese troops along the Vietnamese border were tying down 60 percent of all PAVN units.

[6] See the article in FEER, June 11, 1982, and the *New York Times*, February 9, 1983. Also cf. Justus van der Kroef, "The South China Sea," *International*

The final component of Beijing's strategy was to use its diplomatic influence to isolate Hanoi in the international community. The most visible arena of diplomatic activity was at the United Nations, where China supported the efforts of the ASEAN countries to mobilize support for continued recognition of the government of Democratic Kampuchea as the sole legitimate representative of the Cambodian people. The delegation of Democratic Kampuchea was able to retain its seat in the United Nations, while an annual resolution sponsored by ASEAN demanding the withdrawal of Vietnamese occupation forces from Cambodia and the holding of free general elections under international supervision regularly received majority support in the U.N. General Assembly.

It was not likely that annual votes at the United Nations could force Hanoi to abandon its "special relationship" with the new government in Phnom Penh. So long as Hanoi could count on the support of the Soviet Union and its allies, it need not fear total isolation on the international scene. To Chinese leaders, then, the road to Phnom Penh might lead through Moscow. The idea was not as quixotic as it might have seemed in 1979. In the early 1980s there were indications that Soviet leaders hoped to improve relations with China in order to prevent the formation of a solid Sino-American phalanx in Asia, and Moscow might be induced to reduce its support for Vietnamese policy in Indochina in return for better relations with Beijing. Moreover, there were periodic indications of Soviet unhappiness with Vietnamese belligerence on the Indochina issue, a position that rendered the achievement of other Soviet foreign policy objectives in Southeast Asia more difficult.[7]

Beijing had initiated efforts to open a dialogue with Moscow as early as the spring of 1979. At that time, the main focus of Chinese interest had been on the Sino-Soviet frontier. In the fall of 1982, China and the Soviet Union opened negotiations on a wide-ranging series of issues dividing the two countries. At the talks, Chinese delegates raised three conditions for the establishment of normal relations between the two countries—the pres-

---

Security Review, vol. 7, no. 3 (Fall 1982).

[7] For one account, see FEER, October 15, 1982. Strains in the Soviet-Vietnamese alliance are discussed in Paul Quinn-Judge's article in the *Christian Science Monitor,* March 2, 1982.

ence of Soviet troops on the Chinese frontier, Soviet occupation of Afghanistan, and the Vietnamese occupation of Cambodia. Of the three, China declared, the removal of Vietnamese occupation forces from Cambodia was the most important. China then proposed a five-point plan leading to the gradual withdrawal of Vietnamese forces and the creation of a neutral and independent Cambodia free from external interference.[8]

Beijing's strategy to counter the Vietnamese occupation of Indochina thus represented a multifaceted approach. It was clearly not based on the expectation of immediate results but on the premise that a long-term policy applying political, military, economic, and diplomatic pressure on the Vietnamese would ultimately force Hanoi to accept a compromise commensurate with Chinese foreign policy objectives in Southeast Asia.

Winning Hearts and Minds

Beijing's strategy represented a serious challenge to Hanoi's efforts to consolidate its position in Cambodia and solidify the "special relationship" between the three Indochinese countries. It is not likely, however, that it provoked Hanoi to consider a change in those plans. In the first place, Cambodia was too critical to Vietnamese national security to be bargained away under pressure. In the second place, Vietnamese leaders were probably confident that the anti-Hanoi alliance was inherently vulnerable and would eventually collapse from its internal contradictions. To Hanoi, China and the ASEAN states had little in common except for their momentary distaste for the Vietnamese occupation of Cambodia. Once the PRK had consolidated its position and its popular support within the country, the ASEAN countries could gradually be brought to accept the reality of the Indochinese alliance and even to view it as a useful bulwark against the expansionist plans of the "Han chauvinists" to the north.

Hanoi thus counted on its ability to outwait its adversary, as it had during the previous war against the United States. In

---

[8] For the historical background to the talks, see William E. Griffith, "Sino-Soviet Rapprochement?" *Problems of Communism,* vol. 32 (March-April 1983). China's plan for Cambodia was reported in FEER, March 31, 1983. China had first proposed a three-point plan in July 1981, calling for withdrawal of Vietnamese troops, self-determination for Cambodia, and an international guarantee. See *Beijing Review,* July 20, 1981.

the international arena, its basic objective would be to divide ASEAN from China and to bring the former to accept the ineluctability of Hanoi's "special relationship" with the Indochinese countries. Vietnamese leaders were probably less optimistic that China could be persuaded to readjust its own objectives in the region, but counted on the passage of time to change opinions in Beijing.[9]

In the meantime, Hanoi began to offer cosmetic concessions in the Cambodian dispute while standing firm on the key issue of maintaining the Vietnamese presence. In 1981 Hanoi began to hint that political figures not currently in Cambodia, such as Son Sann and Prince Sihanouk himself, might be able to enter Cambodia and take part in the political process. But they refused to consider any substantive changes in the PRK or the holding of elections to form a new government. They attempted to assuage ASEAN concern over the potential Vietnamese threat to the region by proposing a nonaggression pact with Thailand and pledging to remove Vietnamese occupation forces from the PRK once the threat from China and the Khmer Rouge had been eliminated. On the other hand, Hanoi periodically warned that unless Thailand ceased to provide support for the guerrilla forces operating in Cambodia, it might begin to promote revolution in Thailand.[10]

Hanoi also attempted to use the negotiations process itself to achieve its objectives in the Indochina dispute. At first, it tried to divide ASEAN from China by proposing a conference that would be attended only by the nations within Southeast

---

[9] See, for example, the report in the *Manchester Guardian,* January 21, 1981. According to this source, a top Vietnamese official claimed that some members of the Politburo in Beijing wanted normal relations with the SRV. But China continued to reject Hanoi's overtures. See the *Washington Post,* December 19, 1982.

[10] Hanoi has tried both the carrot and the stick with the Thai. It has offered on many occasions to negotiate a nonaggression treaty with Bangkok and has suggested the creation of a demilitarized zone on both sides of the border. But it has also threatened to lend its support to insurgency activities in Thailand, where it was supporting a new breakaway faction of the traditionally pro-Chinese Thai Communist party. Called the Pak Mai (New Party), the new organization was reportedly founded by pro-Vietnamese elements in 1978. For a report, see John McBeth, "'Foreign Legion' Threat," *FEER,* December 6, 1984. As for Beijing, it has been encountering some problems in preventing the disintegration of the orthodox TCP. See the article in the Bangkok newspaper *Su Angkhot,* November 21, 1982, translated in JPRS 82,574.

Asia. In 1981 the SRV shifted its position, offering a two-stage plan calling for a regional conference to be followed by an international conference attended by other states with interests in the region. After the formation of the CGDK in 1982, Hanoi suggested an international conference attended not only by the ASEAN and the Indochinese states but also by the five major world powers and other neutral countries in the region. Such a conference, it suggested, should consider all international problems in the region, including the U.S. military presence in the Philippines. When the ASEAN countries rejected such a conference on the grounds that it would add legitimacy to the Phnom Penh regime, Hanoi countered that it could take place without representatives from the PRK.

It is doubtful that Vietnamese leaders were optimistic that concessions on such minor issues could lead to meaningful negotiations. But they were useful in keeping the negotiations track alive while the regime concentrated on an issue of more central importance, the situation inside Cambodia. If the Heng Samrin regime could consolidate its internal position and eliminate the threat from the guerrillas, the issue of international recognition would eventually resolve itself. The establishment of the coalition government, however, posed a serious military and political challenge to that effort by creating a vehicle for the mobilization of anti-Vietnamese sentiment in Cambodia and enhancing its stature abroad. To counter such efforts, Hanoi attempted to strengthen the Phnom Penh regime in order to enable it to take greater responsibility over pacification and the administration of the country. At the same time, Vietnamese economic planners began to draw up plans for the economic and social integration of the three Indochinese countries into a single economic unit. One controversial aspect of the plan involved the resettlement of substantial numbers of ethnic Vietnamese in Cambodia. Official sources described the plan as simply part of a broader program adopted in 1975 to resettle millions of Vietnamese from densely populated areas into less settled regions of the country. Critics charged, however, that the plan to settle thousands of Vietnamese in the PRK had political implications as well and served as a means of perpetuating Vietnamese domination over the country. Hanoi and Phnom Penh retorted that most of the Vietnamese were previous residents who had been driven out during the civil war under Lon Nol or the Pol Pot era which had followed it.[11]

A balanced interpretation of this controversy is not easy to achieve. From an economic perspective, the program had potential merit for promoting growth in all three countries. And Hanoi is probably correct in pointing out that many of the new emigrants had lived in Cambodia before the recent troubles. Others may have been South Vietnamese who resettled in Cambodia to escape the harsher realities of socialism at home. Still, the critics are probably correct in seeing political motives behind the plan. Vietnamese leaders undoubtedly view the program as a means of facilitating their effort to integrate Cambodia into a larger political and economic unit dominated by the SRV. Whatever the motives, Hanoi was taking a risk. While there appears to be little open resentment of the Vietnamese on the part of the local population, there is little doubt that such ethnic suspicion exists under the surface and could be exacerbated by the presence of large numbers of the more dominant Vietnamese, particularly when they occupy positions of authority in society. For the time being, however, Hanoi probably felt it had little choice. Because of the lack of trained Khmer, Vietnamese were introduced as advisers in the bureaucracy and in the armed services. Because of the inexperience of the PRK armed forces, Vietnamese troops performed the primary pacification duties and provided security for the capital. According to refugee sources, the entire operation was overseen by a shadowy branch of the VCP Central Committee known as B-68.[12]

In the meantime, the Vietnamese also attempted to shore up their defenses against the Chinese threat inside the SRV. The border region in the north was strengthened as the regime attempted to turn over primary responsibility to the local administration by creating so-called combat districts that could carry the primary burden of defense against a possible external attack. To remove the primary sources of unrest in Vietnamese society, the regime sought to promote economic growth, and relaxed the

---

[11] For press reports on the issue, see the *Christian Science Monitor,* May 13, 1983; *Vietnam Courier* (November 1983); and *People's Daily* (cited in *Survey of World Broadcasts, Far East,* August 5, 1983). For an interpretive essay, see Murray Hiebert, "Cambodia and Vietnam: Costs of the Alliance," *Indochina Issues,* no. 46 (May 1984). According to Hiebert, about one-third of all ethnic Vietnamese residing in the PRK had not lived there previously.

[12] The *New York Times,* October 9, 1982; *FEER,* October 15, 1982.

tempo of socialist transformation. At the same time, however, it relentlessly pursued potential sources of dissidence among the tribal minorities, overseas Chinese, the sects, and other "counterrevolutionary elements," and attempted to weed out "Maoist elements" within the party, the administration, and the armed forces.[13]

To curb the lingering influence of Chinese ideas in Vietnam, Hanoi launched a major campaign to discredit Maoism as a reactionary and chauvinist ideology that betrayed the true principles of Marxism-Leninism. China, said the 1979 White Paper, had betrayed the sacred concept of proletarian internationalism. The aim of Beijing's foreign policy was to conquer Southeast Asia and ultimately the entire world. Mao Zedong and his colleagues were driven by "big nation expansionism and hegemonistic designs" and wanted to seize Southeast Asia for its raw materials and settle China's excess population in empty areas of Thailand and Laos. In reality, taunted Hanoi, Beijing was "big but not strong," and the Vietnamese operation in Cambodia had thrown Chinese policy into confusion and demonstrated its essential passivity.[14]

The regime also criticized Chinese domestic policy as a betrayal of the true principles of Marxism-Leninism. Maoism itself was not a proletarian ideology but a combination of peasant, petty bourgeois, and feudal concepts. Instead of relying on the leading role of the party, China had deified the thought and personality of Mao Zedong. Instead of seeking its source and strength in the working class, the CCP had created a form of "peasant communism." According to a recent article by a Vietnamese historian, the two Communist parties had taken different paths as early as the 1920s. Where the Vietnamese sent party members to the

---

[13] For one report, see Nong Quoc Chan, "Oppose the Enemy's Psychological Warfare at the Sino-Vietnamese Border," *Tap Chi Cong San,* no. 6 (June 1982), translated in JPRS 81,758. Hanoi's counterefforts are recorded in Bui Nguyen, "Political work at places fighting enchroachment and occupation by the enemy," *Tap Chi Quan Doi Nhan Dan* (September 1982), translated in JPRS 82,501. According to one Vietnamese source, "Maoist" sentiment within the VCP existed primarily among ethnic Chinese members of the party. For the most part, he said, this problem has been eliminated, and most of the remaining Chinese in the SRV are loyal to the regime and its policies. Interview with Nguyen Quang Du, December 7, 1985.

[14] *The Truth,* p. 5. See also Nhuan Vu, "Some Matters Concerning Chinese Military Strategy," *Tap Chi Cong San,* no. 8 (August 1982).

factories to learn from the working class, the CCP based its power on the village, and later sent Chinese intellectuals to rural areas to learn from the peasants. And where the Vietnamese had absorbed the critical importance of political struggle in the Vietnamese revolution, Mao glorified the idea of violence per se and taught that "power comes out of the barrel of a gun." Such ideas, claimed Hanoi, led China astray from the true path of Marxism-Leninism and to the "great chaos" of the Great Proletarian Cultural Revolution."[15]

There are indeed significant differences between Chinese communism and its Vietnamese counterpart. Where both parties contend that Marxist doctrine must be adapted to the conditions within each individual country, the Vietnamese are dedicated adherents to Leninist orthodoxy, and have tended to seek answers to local problems in classical precedent. The Chinese, by contrast, have been much more innovative in seeking indigenous solutions to the problems of applying Marxist precepts to Chinese society. That generalization is as true of the current leadership under Deng Xiaoping as it was previously under Mao Zedong. The explanation lies at least partly in history. China, of course, has traditionally seen its own culture as unique, while the Vietnamese have often looked abroad for models of political and social development. It is an interesting subject worthy of further analysis.

War and Diplomacy

By the mid-1980s both Beijing and Hanoi had appeared to settle on a long-range strategy to outwait their adversaries. For the time being the focus was on feint, on flanking movements and on psychological warfare, rather than on direct attack. Inside Cambodia the Vietnamese moved painstakingly to improve the overall capacity and effectiveness of the PRK in eliminating

---

[15] The limitations of space prevent a detailed analysis of this issue. Some of Hanoi's charges represent a gross distortion of the actual strategies pursued by each party. Yet there is an element of truth in Vietnamese criticism of the unorthodox and unstable tendencies within the CCP. See Van Tao, "Nhung net khac nhua giua cach mang Viet Nam va cach mang Trung Quoc" [The differences between the Vietnamese and Chinese revolutions], *Nghien Cuu Lich Su,* no. 190 (January-February 1980). For another perspective, cf. Hoang Tung, "The world situation and the foreign policy of our Party and State," *Giao Duc Ly Luan* [Education and theory], no. 5. (September-October 1982), translated in JPRS 82,735.

the threat posed by the CGDK. China countered by providing increased military assistance to all factions in the coalition, by maintaining pressure on the Sino-Vietnamese border, and by threatening to launch a "second lesson" to punish Hanoi. In the diplomatic arena both moved to shore up their own support while surreptitiously courting their adversaries. China attempted to bolster faltering ASEAN self-confidence by increasing the level of its assistance to the coalition forces and urging Washington to do the same. At the same time, it continued its efforts to pry Moscow from its support for the SRV. In the meantime, Hanoi probed for cracks in the anti-Vietnamese alliance, offering minor concessions in an effort to court the sympathy of lukewarm elements such as Indonesia and Australia while openly seeking normalization talks with the United States. It also continued to signal its desire for a reconciliation with Beijing, proposing the signing of a treaty of peaceful coexistence between the two countries. The PRC made no public reply, but rumors circulated in 1983 that Chinese and Vietnamese negotiators had held secret talks in Bucharest, or in Beijing.[16]

To many observers the Cambodian dispute had reached a stalemate. Yet both Hanoi and Beijing recognized that the situation inside Cambodia was a key factor in shaping the outcome of the struggle. The success of China's strategy depended, above all, on its ability to maintain the CGDK as a credible force and an alternative to the Hanoi-dominated regime in Phnom Penh. If Hanoi could demonstrate that the coalition could not succeed, it could lure ASEAN into a settlement and perhaps even compel China to abandon its own strategy. For a time, Hanoi had taken a relatively cautious approach to the task of eliminating the forces in the anti-Vietnamese coalition, possibly fearing that a more aggressive effort might antagonize the ASEAN countries and make a diplomatic solution more difficult to achieve. But the brightening fortunes of the CGDK, and the resultant improvement in its stature on the international scene, along with the persistent failure of Vietnamese diplomatic initiatives to achieve a breakthrough in the negotiating deadlock, apparently exhausted the patience of party leaders in Hanoi. The regime may also have been nervous at the prospect of improved Sino-Soviet relations stemming from the scheduled visit to Beijing of

---

[16] For a report on the holding of secret talks, see FEER, March 10, 1983.

Soviet Vice Premier Arkhipov in late 1984.

These disquieting factors were undoubtedly raised at the party's Seventh Plenum held in mid-December. The outcome of that discussion was soon reflected on the battlefield in Cambodia. In December and January, PAVN units launched their annual dry season offensive on guerrilla emplacements along the Thai border. The operation was more aggressive than in previous years. The Vietnamese seized several base camps and drove the guerrilla forces and their camp followers across the frontier into Thailand. There was little mystery about Hanoi's intentions. If Vietnamese troops could impose a serious defeat on the coalition forces, it would not only reduce the security threat to the Phnom Penh regime, it would also discredit the coalition as a potential alternative to the PRK and reduce support for it on the international scene.

Having attempted to achieve a significant transformation of the balance of forces inside Cambodia, Hanoi then launched new diplomatic initiatives to promote a peace settlement. A communiqué issued at the semiannual meeting of the Indochinese foreign ministers held in January presented a new proposal for the resolution of the dispute, promising a total withdrawal of Vietnamese forces and the holding of free elections in the presence of foreign observers *following* the complete elimination of the Pol Pot clique. The foreign ministers of the three countries also voiced their desire for improved relations with both the United States and the PRC. According to the communiqué

> the three Indochinese peoples have invariably treasured their time-honoured friendship with the Chinese people and always looked forward to an early restoration of this friendship. A relationship of friendship and cooperation between Viet Nam, Laos, and Kampuchea on the one hand and the People's Republic of China on the other, would constitute a factor of extreme importance for peace and stability in Southeast Asia. What matters most is that both sides should show good will. In that spirit, the Lao People's Democratic Republic and the People's Republic of Kampuchea fully support the endeavors of the Socialist Republic of Viet Nam to restore peace in the Viet Nam border regions and to resume the Sino-Vietnamese negotiations for the normalization of their relations.[17]

---

[17] Bulletin of the Permanent Mission to the United Nations of the SRV (PMUN), January 17–18, 1985.

Hanoi's aggressive new stance had immediate repercussions in Cambodia where it not only damaged the military position but, according to press reports, also undermined the morale of the coalition forces. The Vietnamese diplomatic barrage, however, had less success. While the results of the offensive provoked a reevaluation of the coalition's strategic assumptions and may have caused some soul-searching in ASEAN capitals, it did not result in a breakthrough in the negotiations deadlock. ASEAN dismissed the new plan as ambiguous and a rehash of old proposals, while neither Washington nor Beijing reacted favorably to Hanoi's appeal for improved relations. But the offensive did have salutary consequences for the SRV in forcing its adversaries on the defensive. China initially issued a tough response to the Vietnamese border campaign, and on January 19 Foreign Minister Wu Xueqian (Wu Hsueh-ch'ien) warned in Singapore that if Vietnam did not cease its aggressive activities China would administer its long publicized "second lesson." In ensuing weeks, however, Beijing did little to back up Wu's words. Although armed shipments to the coalition forces increased and Chinese spokesmen stated bluntly that they would not tolerate the elimination of the Khmer Rouge, there were no reports of a significant movement of Chinese troops or military material into the border area; and Chinese military operations along the frontier, despite the usual charges on both sides, were apparently smaller than in previous years.[18]

Beijing's failure to administer its "second lesson" aroused surprise and some concern in ASEAN capitals, where observers openly speculated that China had abandoned its policy of using military force as an instrument of policy in the Cambodian dispute. Beijing attempted to put a good face on the situation, remarking that China would act when the occasion required it and pointing out that the new situation would ultimately work to the benefit of the rebel forces in Cambodia, since the Vietnamese had been forced to place the bulk of their troops along the border, thus opening up the interior for guerrilla operations and giving the Khmer Rouge a new opportunity to improve its links with the masses. Still, Beijing's cautious reaction to the Viet-

---

[18] For Vietnamese complaints of Chinese provocations along the border, see the statement by the Ministry of Foreign Affairs in PMUN, February 2 and May 20, 1985.

namese offensive appeared to be a clear indication that Chinese leaders were reevaluating their strategy, or at least their tactics, in the Cambodia conflict. Some observers speculated that Beijing had concluded that because of the increased number of Vietnamese front-line troops near the frontier—now reportedly numbering 19 divisions compared with only 12 in 1979—a "second lesson" would not only be more militarily hazardous but would also play into the hands of the Vietnamese by delaying China's program of economic modernization.[19]

There may have been other reasons as well. In the 1980s, as has been the case since the early 1950s, China's strategy toward Vietnam has consistently been formulated in the context of its overall foreign policy objectives, and particularly its relations with the Great Powers. With negotiations with the Soviet Union now at a delicate stage, Chinese leaders may have hoped to send a signal to Moscow that the dispute with Vietnam would not be permitted to set back prospects for an improvement in Sino-Soviet relations. According to one source, CCP General Secretary General Hu Yaobang's message of condolences on the death of Konstantin Chernenko in March 1985 did not mention Beijing's "three obstacles" to a normalization of relations. At a new round of Sino-Soviet talks the following month, Deng Xiaoping reportedly confirmed these signs of a softening of Beijing's position when he remarked that while the "three obstacles" still remained as an impediment to improved Sino-Soviet relations, they could be removed "gradually." Moreover, he added, the USSR could "still retain the bases provided by Vietnam."[20] If such is the case, China may have now decided to test the diplomatic waters in its search for an exit from the Cambodian impasse.

During the remainder of the year, the SRV continued its diplomatic barrage. On several occasions Vietnamese leaders signaled their desire for an improvement in relations with China. In August the semiannual meeting of the Indochinese foreign ministers registered an interest in Malaysia's proposal for "proximity talks" between the two sides through intermediaries and announced that Vietnamese troops would complete their withdrawal from the PRK by 1990. The foreign ministers indicated

---

[19] See the reports in FEER, March 14 and May 30, 1985.
[20] See Richard Nations, "Great Leap Sideways," in FEER, May 30, 1985.

their willingness to open talks "with various opposition groups or individuals" provided that they first abandoned the Khmer Rouge. In November the SRV formally agreed to hold direct talks with Khmer Rouge without the participation of Pol Pot and Ieng Sary, but said that the final outcome of the talks must result in the dismantling of the Khmer Rouge organization. There was no immediate response to these initiatives. Some ASEAN sources indicated their interest in "proximity talks," but China registered its disapproval of the idea, reiterating its determination to continue providing support for the CGDK. At the same time, Beijing reportedly stepped up its pressure on the Sino-Vietnamese frontier and rejected a Vietnamese proposal for negotiations to settle the border dispute.[21]

Conclusions

Since 1979 both Hanoi and Beijing have pursued a long-term strategy in Cambodia. While there has been some movement on the diplomatic scene, neither has yet indicated a serious interest in exploring a compromise solution, and each appears determined to test the patience of the other. China has counted on its ability to impose a variety of pressures to force Hanoi to change its policy and possibly to provoke a change in leadership as the generation of Le Duan gradually departs the scene. The Vietnamese, no strangers to the concept of protracted war, have attempted to match the Chinese at their own game, counting on the passage of time to drive fissures in the anti-Hanoi alliance and induce international acceptance of the new regime in Phnom Penh.

Can Hanoi outwait Beijing in Cambodia? Both, of course, regularly employ patience as an integral component in their foreign policy, and it would be foolhardy to attempt a long-term projection here. From the present vantage point, however, it appears that Hanoi has a number of significant advantages in this war of nerves. In Cambodia the pacification effort is proceeding on schedule. Predictions by Vietnamese leaders that Vietnamese occupation troops can be removed by 1990 do not seem unrealistic. While the cost of that occupation is not insignificant, it is

---

[21] The *New York Times,* January 5, 1986; FEER, October 26, 1985. For the current SRV statement on the Sino-Vietnamese relationship, see the interview with Le Duc Tho in *Vietnam Courier* (June 1985), pp. 13–14.

probably bearable.[22] In the meantime, the centrifugal strains within the anti-Hanoi alliance are likely to intensify and may drive ASEAN to seek a negotiated settlement. Although ASEAN support is not essential to the success of China's strategy, since Beijing's main concern is its relationship with Thailand, the breakdown of the PRC-ASEAN alliance would still have serious repercussions for the former's strategy to isolate Hanoi within the international community and could raise problems in its relationship with Bangkok.[23]

The Vietnamese, however, cannot afford to feel totally secure about their current position or their future prospects in Indochina. In the first place, China is a formidable adversary; and although it has chosen not to apply military force to achieve its objectives in Indochina, it has the capacity to cause Hanoi severe problems in consolidating its power in Indochina and, equally serious, in its effort to spur economic development at home. Even if Beijing should appear to acquiesce temporarily in Vietnamese domination over Laos and Cambodia, it is not likely that Chinese leaders will easily abandon their long-term goal of bringing Hanoi to heel and reasserting their influence in Indochina.[24]

Hanoi must also worry about the impact of Sino-Soviet negotiations and the evolving relationship among the Great Powers on its own interests in Southeast Asia. Up to now Moscow has provided dependable support for Vietnam in its struggle against Beijing. Although there have been occasional signs of Soviet dissatisfaction with Vietnamese policy in Cambodia, the Soviet Union has publicly backed Hanoi on the issue and has refrained from open criticism of its ally. In recent months it has offered to take part in an international conference on Cambodia

---

[22] It is generally assumed that military expenses consume about 60 percent of the total SRV state budget. For a recent estimate, see the AFP report in FBIS, volume 4, September 12, 1983. Much of the cost, of course, is borne by the USSR. One Vietnamese source told me recently that Hanoi sees Vietnam-Laos relations as a model for the future relations between Vietnam and the PRK. According to press reports, there are currently several thousand Vietnam troops in Laos. Interview with Nguyen Quang Du, December 7, 1985.

[23] Interview with Chinese diplomatic official, Washington, D.C., March 8, 1985.

[24] According to Sihanouk, Deng Xiaoping told him that China would help the Cambodians drive Vietnam out of the country even if it took twenty years. *War and Hope*, p. 109.

and to serve as a guarantor for a possible Indochina settlement. But Hanoi cannot forget that the USSR, like China, has on past occasions been prone to sacrifice the needs of the Vietnamese revolution on the altar of its own foreign policy concerns. A Soviet bargain with China at the expense of Vietnamese interests in Indochina is not out of the question.[25]

Nor can the Vietnamese ignore the evidence of a rising level of anti-Vietnamese sentiment inside Cambodia itself. While most observers agree that Hanoi possesses the military power to maintain its position in Cambodia indefinitely, the force of Khmer nationalism represents an intangible element that the continuing presence of Vietnamese troops and advisers can only foster.

The Vietnamese appear to be fully conscious of this problem, and to all appearances they are making a serious effort to reduce the visibility of their presence in Cambodia. Western residents in Phnom Penh tend to agree that there are fewer Vietnamese in the capital than in past years, while PRK officials contend that Vietnamese advisers are gradually being withdrawn, providing more responsibilities for civilian and military officials of the PRK. Cambodian troops have reportedly been assigned increasing security functions along the Thai border, and settlers from the interior have been moved up to the frontier to form a network of combat villages to seal off the area from future infiltration. Vietnamese troops still bear the primary responsibility for security in Phnom Penh, but one Cambodian official noted proudly that whereas the PAVN were until recently assigned sentry duties at Pochentong airport, that responsibility is now handled by soldiers of the PRK.[26]

For the moment, then, Hanoi appears to be confident that it can maintain its position in Cambodia after the removal of Vietnamese troops through a series of interlocking relationships knitting all three Indochinese countries into a close political, economic, and social unit directed from Hanoi. It also is counting on its ability to exert influence over the small and still sha-

---

[25] For example, Moscow reportedly told Hanoi it would go ahead with the Sino-Soviet normalization talks despite the rising level of violence on the Sino-Vietnamese border. See FEER, March 21, 1985.

[26] Comment by Cambodian foreign ministry official, Phnom Penh, December 19, 1985.

dowy KPRP, several of whose key members have been reportedly sent for training to Vietnam or the USSR. Even here, however, the Vietnamese cannot afford the luxury of relaxing their vigilance. While there are no current signs of restiveness within the Phnom Penh regime, there are a number of centrifugal forces in the region, and future leaders of the PRK may well be tempted to fish in the muddy waters of international politics to achieve a degree of breathing space in their relationship with their insistent patron.[27]

---

[27] One possible example of this was the firing of KPRP General Secretary Pen Sovan in late 1981. While it was officially stated that Pen Sovan had resigned for reasons of health, there were persistent rumors that he may have sought to approach Moscow in order to gain leverage with Hanoi.

VI

The Road to Reconciliation

As this study has attempted to demonstrate, a number of factors have contributed to the current tension in Sino-Vietnamese relations. The legacy of the war, the territorial dispute, the issue of the overseas Chinese, and ideological differences have all played a role in provoking the confrontation that burst into open conflict in early 1979. But it is the Cambodian problem, and the geopolitical factors that surround it, that has become the key issue in the dispute. Most if not all of the other sources of contention could be resolved, given an atmosphere of good will on both sides. The territorial dispute, for example, should not prove to be an insurmountable barrier to improved relations. Both China and Vietnam have demonstrated a willingness to compromise on border questions in negotiations with other countries in the area. As for the issue of Vietnamese mistreatment of the overseas Chinese, Beijing has frequently ignored mistreatment of Chinese nationals in several Southeast Asian countries when its overall foreign policy interests demanded it.[1]

In actuality, however, even the rivalry over influence in Indochina is only a surface manifestation of a deeper issue dividing the two countries. Behind the Cambodian dispute is the broader problem of placing Sino-Vietnamese relations on a new footing with the end of the Vietnam War in 1975. China, still recovering from the humiliation at the hands of the imperialist powers at the end of the last century, appears determined to re-

---

[1] Recent examples are the period of the anti-Chinese riots during the Malaysian Emergency in the early 1970s and the continued restrictions on activities by ethnic Chinese residents in Suharto's Indonesia. Only during the height of the Cultural Revolution, when Chinese communities in Southeast Asia were the source of radical activities promoting Mao Zedong Thought, did Beijing make an issue of official treatment of Chinese nationals.

store its traditional role in Southeast Asia by creating a string of submissive client states along its southern frontier. Vietnam, sensitive to centuries of Chinese domination and just emerging from a generation of civil war and division, is equally determined to reassert its independence and realize its own national destiny.

The relationship is not an unfamiliar one in contemporary politics. Even Great Powers like the Soviet Union and the United States have occasionally experienced problems in enforcing their will on obstinate smaller neighbors. Cuba and Yugoslavia are only the most prominent examples in our own day. But the issue has a particular acuteness in the case of China and Vietnam. Territorial contiguity, close ethnic and cultural ties, and a long and complex relationship stretching back over two thousand years, have enmeshed the two societies into a web of common historical experiences and attitudes that can impede mutual understanding and the making of a new start.

Since the dispute broke into the open nearly a decade ago, there have been few grounds for optimism that an early solution was possible. In recent months, however, there have been some indications of possible movement in both capitals. Beijing's failure to launch attacks along the Sino-Vietnamese border in response to the Vietnamese dry season offensive in Cambodia led to speculation that Chinese leaders were having second thoughts about their strategy of seeking to influence Hanoi through military intimidation. In turn, Vietnamese peace feelers suggest the possibility that Hanoi may be ready to accept a compromise in the interests of reaching a settlement.

Too much, however, should not be made of such tantalizing hints of potential rapprochement. To all indications, the security objectives of the two sides remain mutually incompatible, while the legacy of bitterness surrounding the relationship remains too deep to permit the emergence of a spirit of compromise. Such, at any rate, appears to be the current perception in Hanoi. Although official sources sometimes imply cautious optimism that China can be brought to change its ways, the current Vietnamese leadership is probably convinced that the dispute will be a long and difficult one. Analyses of the dispute in the Vietnamese press portray Beijing's current policy as only the contemporary manifestation of a historical Chinese effort to dominate Vietnam and, through Vietnam, all of Southeast Asia. While there may be an element of hyperbole in such charges, there seems little doubt that the current leadership in Hanoi has harbored deep suspicions of Chinese motives since the early 1950s and that such suspicions have intensified since the end of the Vietnam War.[2]

If such is the case, the Vietnamese have probably concluded that the Chinese effort to achieve a dominant position in Southeast Asia must be treated as a virtually permanent feature of the regional scene. This perspective emerged clearly in a brief exposition of Chinese foreign policy given recently by Hanoi's deputy minister for foreign affairs, Vo Dong Giang. Asked if there were any indications of a change in Chinese policy, he replied that current policy shifts in Beijing appear to be tactical rather than strategic. At first, he explained, China attempted to intimidate Vietnam through military coercion. When that tactic failed, Chinese leaders shifted to a multifaceted "cold war" approach designed to weaken Vietnam internally and isolate it on the world scene. This too, he said, has now failed. A renewed attempt to bring Vietnam into line by means of a "second lesson," however, would be both risky from a military point of view and costly to China's domestic goals. Chinese leaders may now be considering the adoption of a new policy of "peaceful coexistence" which—as in the case of the relationship between the Soviet Union and the United States—still retains the primary objective of isolating and ultimately destroying the enemy.

But this new policy, he stated, also poses risks to Beijing, for if China agrees to hold bilateral talks with the SRV it could precipitate a rush to negotiations among the ASEAN countries and lead to a collapse of the anti-Hanoi alliance over Cambodia.

---

[2] Evidence of tension in the relationship between the two Communist parties prior to 1949 is tenuous. Sources in Hanoi have little information on the matter, although one veteran party leader pointed out that Ho Chi Minh criticized the concept of peasant leadership over the revolution during a speech in Moscow in 1923, thus suggesting that Vietnamese party leaders could not have approved of the "peasant communism" practiced by the CCP during the 1930s. Interview with Ha Huy Giap, director of the Ho Chi Minh Museum, Hanoi, December 10, 1985. For the moment, firm evidence on intraparty relations prior to 1949 is lacking. Professor Van Tao, director of the Institute of History, may be correct, however, in speculating that because of bitter past experience, ICP leaders were "vigilant" to the possibility that the CCP would resume the practice of "big nation chauvinism" practiced by their imperial predecessors. Interview with Van Tao, Hanoi, December 10, 1985.

Chinese leaders are therefore caught in a quandary and would like to adjust their relation with Vietnam quietly while at the same time reassuring their allies that their hardline policy on Cambodia has not changed. Hanoi therefore dismisses the "mixed signals" that it is currently receiving from Beijing as indicating tactical uncertainly rather than the portent of a major shift in regional strategy. China will only change its policy, he predicted, when its leaders become convinced that they cannot achieve their objective of establishing hegemony over Southeast Asia.[3]

Given this perspective, Hanoi's insistence that its treaty relationship with Moscow has become a "cornerstone of Vietnamese foreign policy" becomes comprehensible. Vo Dong Giang concedes that the treaty complicates Vietnamese efforts to improve relations with China and the nations of the West. But he counters that recent experience has convinced Vietnamese leaders that close ties with the Soviet Union are necessary to protect the SRV from bullying by China or other aggressive powers. The relationship with the USSR is therefore a strategic one and will not be affected by improving relations with other states. If that is the case, the treaty, in present circumstances, is not negotiable.[4]

Will Hanoi's strategy succeed? Given the current trends in the region, Vietnamese leaders must be reasonably confident that their efforts will eventually bear fruit. If, as now seems probable, the coalition government collapses and the PRK is able to consolidate its authority in Cambodia, the anti-Hanoi alliance between China and the ASEAN states may well break down. While ASEAN leaders may be reluctant to grant their imprimature to the process, the Vietnamese "special relationship" in

---

[3] Interview with Deputy Foreign Minister Vo Dong Giang, Hanoi, December 14, 1985.

[4] Ibid. For an earlier and equally authoritative exposition of this view, see the interview of Le Duc Tho in *Vietnam Courier* (June 1985). Vietnamese leaders may not be particularly sanguine over the prospects for improved relations with Washington. According to Mr. Vo Dong Giang, the Cambodian issue is only a pretext in the U.S. refusal to normalize relations with the SRV. American policy in Southeast Asia, he asserted, is based on collusion with Beijing to maintain the status quo in the region. The time will come, he predicted, when the United States will have to reconsider the implications of this policy in terms of its regional and global interests.

Indochina will gradually become accepted as an ineluctable reality on the regional scene. Should the ASEAN consensus on opposing Hanoi's hegemony in Indochina collapse, Western nations will be tempted to normalize relations with the SRV as a means of promoting regional reconciliation and defusing tensions in the area. Given the current global situation, of course, such a rapprochement is likely to be limited. It is one of the drawbacks of Hanoi's current strategy that so long as the SRV is identified closely with Soviet interests in the area, relations with the United States and its close allies are likely to be strained. Vietnamese leaders are well aware of the costs of their alliance with Moscow, but they appear willing to bear the burden.

China will be a tougher nut to crack. Vo Dong Giang's analysis of the policy options in Beijing is probably close to the mark. While the success of the recent Vietnamese border offensive and the danger signs of a possible collapse of the anti-Hanoi alliance have probably shaken the confidence of Chinese leaders and may have prompted a high-level policy review in Beijing, the risks to China of a change in strategy may appear to outweigh the potential advantages. While there may be some sentiment among Chinese policy makers to seek a modus vivendi with Hanoi that would end the current impasse and permit a greater degree of concentration on domestic construction, others may argue that the current policy is less risky and imposes higher costs on Vietnam than on the PRC. In any event, the Chinese are resourceful and persistent and will not readily accept defeat in an area of such intrinsic importance to their own security requirements. It is unlikely, therefore, that Beijing's recent setbacks will lead to a fundamental shift in Chinese strategy in the region. From the outset, that strategy has been long-term in its conceptualization, and the rationale behind it—that persistent pressure will eventually force a change of policy or leadership in Hanoi—has not yet been disproved. At the moment, Chinese efforts are focused on improving relations with Moscow and on modernizing the domestic economy. Should the former succeed, Hanoi will be deprived of the protective mantle of its powerful sponsor. Should the latter succeed, China will be in a position to restate its claim early in the next century.

The Vietnamese insist that they are prepared to meet the Chinese threat, from whatever direction. They are evidently prepared to go to considerable lengths to demonstrate their value to the Soviet Union. As for the economic challenge presented by the current modernization efforts in China, Vo Dong Giang replied that one justification for Hanoi's current domestic strategy is precisely to create conditions favorable for peaceful economic construction. "We will deal with the Chinese," he said, "the way they deal with us." First, he added, it is necessary to convince Beijing that Vietnam cannot be conquered by military means.[5]

It is understandable that the veteran leadership currently in power in Hanoi should conclude from historical experience that military strength is more important to national security than economic growth. During the Vietnam War, Hanoi was able to build a modern and powerful military establishment on the basis of a relatively primitive economic base, thanks to aid from its socialist allies. Such calculations, however, may be misplaced for the period ahead, given the volatility of Cold War relationships. A reorientation of Soviet strategy in Asia, while not likely for the immediate future, is a distinct possibility over the longer term. Even should Moscow continue to see the value of the current relationship with Hanoi, its willingness to bankroll Vietnamese security requirements may decline with time, particularly if Vietnamese and Soviet interests in the area do not coincide. Should the Vietnamese be deprived of the Soviet protective umbrella, they will be forced to rely increasingly on their own devices. It is a scenario guaranteed to cause nightmares in Hanoi.

Vietnamese sources concede the importance of economic strength to national security, but they are evidently not willing to grant it equal priority. While domestic policy today emphasizes the use of material incentives to encourage growth in both the industrial and agricultural sectors, there is no indication that military expenditures will be substantially reduced to provide increased resources to economic construction. One official at the Institute of International Relations predicted that even if Sino-Vietnamese relations should improve, defense costs would continue to remain high for the foreseeable future.[6]

If this analysis is correct, it is unlikely that there will be a major breakthrough in Sino-Vietnamese relations in the near future. It should not be assumed, however, that there are no fac-

---

[5] Ibid.

[6] Interview with Nguyen Guang Du, deputy director of the Institute of International Relations, Hanoi, December 9, 1985.

tors leading toward a possible resolution of the conflict. In the first place, much of the antagonism toward Vietnam felt in Beijing has stemmed from insecurity inherited from the imperialist era and from the recent fear of Chinese leaders that Vietnam will be transformed into an instrument for the realization of Moscow's hegemonistic designs in Asia. If China's modernization effort succeeds, and if the current trend toward improving Sino-Soviet relations continues, China will feel more secure, and less sensitive to the threat to its southern flank. In the meantime, the increasingly active U.S. role in the region has provided China with an additional counterforce to growing Soviet power in the region. Recent statements from Chinese sources that the Soviet presence in Vietnam is directed more against the United States than against the PRC may be partly based on wishful thinking, but they also represent a growing recognition by Chinese leaders that the thrust of Soviet policy in Asia is directed not primarily at the PRC, but at the United States. With Washington now more actively involved in the affairs of the region, China can afford to assume a more benign attitude toward the Vietnamese role in the area.

As for Hanoi, it is not unlikely that as the present veteran leadership in Hanoi departs from the scene, the extreme sensitivity to national defense that has understandably dominated Vietnamese foreign policy during recent decades may gradually decline, giving way to a new generation of leaders more inclined to grasp the close relationship between economic development and the realization of true national security. To the degree that economic concerns assume greater importance in Beijing and Hanoi, both countries will find persuasive reasons to seek out new areas of cooperation and mutual reconciliation.[7]

One logical corollary of that process would be a gradual reduction in Vietnamese dependence on the Soviet Union. There are several reasons for this. In the first place, the current dependency relationship with Moscow represents an affront to Vietnamese pride and limits Hanoi's flexibility in adopting an in-

---

[7] There are reports that the Sixth Party Congress, now scheduled to take place in the last quarter of 1986, will announce a major overhaul of the party and government leadership. The composition of that leadership, and the implications for domestic and foreign policy, cannot yet be predicted. Many foreign observers assume, however, that the new leadership will be compelled to devote increased attention and resources to economic development.

dependent foreign policy. Although spokesmen for the regime insist that the Soviet Union does not possess military bases on Vietnamese soil, several sources attest to the fact that Hanoi has only limited authority over Soviet military activities at Da Nang and Cam Ranh Bay, a fact that must be galling to the proud Vietnamese. Moreover, the Soviet presence also complicates Hanoi's efforts to achieve a measure of reconciliation with its non-Communist neighbors and to promote the creation of a "zone of peace, freedom, and neutrality" (ZOPFAN) in Southeast Asia. Finally, the close economic tie with CMEA is of dubious benefit to the Vietnamese. The Soviet Union is not a particularly reassuring model for economic development—as some of the younger and more sophisticated Vietnamese technocrats appear to be well aware—and has relatively little to offer a backward Asian country striving to transform itself into a technologically advanced industrial society. While the current leadership espouses a strictly orthodox Leninist posture on economic policy, some of its younger technocrats appear to be deeply curious about China's recent economic successes. They cannot be unconscious of the fact that much of that success is due to Beijing's increasingly close political and economic ties with the West. It is not impossible that at some future date the Vietnamese will once again be tempted to imitate the Chinese model.[8]

There are, then, areas of possible conciliation in the tortuous Sino-Vietnamese tangle. It will require a measure of understanding and good will on each side. China must come to terms with the existence of Vietnam as a powerful and independent neighbor with the capacity and will to play an influential role in the affairs of the region. In fact, there is still an element of "Greater Han chauvinism" in Beijing's view of its smaller neighbors in Southeast Asia, and the Vietnamese are not alone in

---

[8] I do not wish to imply that conditions for economic growth and technological modernization are identical in China and Vietnam. Vietnamese policy makers will undoubtedly find that any economic strategy, whether borrowed from the USSR, from China, or from the West, will have to be adapted to local circumstances. But today as in the past, the two countries are linked together by geography, history, and cultural experience; and although Hanoi is publicly hostile to the "revisionist" strategy followed by the current leadership in Beijing, future Vietnamese leaders may be tempted to test its applicability in their own country.

pointing this out. China must recognize that it has never been a dominant political force in mainland Southeast Asia and that its true concern in the area, as Jay Taylor has remarked, is security rather than preeminence.[9] Beijing has tacitly conceded that fact, at least for the moment, by abandoning military force as an instrument to drive the Vietnamese out of Indochina.

For its part, Hanoi must recognize that China does possess legitimate security concerns in Southeast Asia and cannot be expected to tolerate a hostile presence on its southern frontier. It must eventually adjust its relationship with Moscow accordingly. The Vietnamese cannot be expected to denounce their current political and military links with the Soviet Union simply for the hypothetical possibility of improved relations with Beijing. Moscow is too important as a trump card to guarantee future Chinese good behavior, and the Vietnamese are well aware that small countries need powerful sponsors in a dangerous world. But Hanoi would clearly benefit from a better relationship with China, and with the United States, particularly if it provided more independence from the suffocating Soviet embrace. The process will not be an easy one, for Vietnam today is increasingly dependent upon the USSR for its economic well-being as well as for its national survival. But there are corresponding benefits to a more independent posture in international affairs, and sooner or later the Vietnamese will be tempted to take advantage of them.

Such a reconciliation will not come easily, for the legacy of distrust runs deep. But the historical record of Sino-Vietnamese relations is marked by periods of cooperation as well as conflict, and the arguments for improved relations are persuasive on both sides. While an element of uneasiness and distrust is likely to remain, the demands of reality will militate against the perpetuation of hostility.

What would be the consequences of improving Sino-Vietnamese relations for the United States and for other states in the region? This is a difficult question to answer because of all the unpredictable factors involved. What kind of leadership will emerge in Hanoi and Beijing in coming decades and what kinds of strategies will they pursue in foreign affairs? Will the current level of prosperity in many countries of Asia persist, or will ad-

---

[9] *China and Southeast Asia,* p. 385.

verse global trends lead to recession and political instability in the region? Will China's emergence as a regional economic power lead it to seek political dominance in Southeast Asia, as Hanoi fears, or herald a new era of conciliation with its neighbors? How will the Beijing-Moscow-Washington triangle evolve in coming years?

There are, then, no guarantees that improved Sino-Vietnamese relations would work to the benefit of the peoples in the region as a whole. It is not impossible that Beijing and Hanoi once again could cooperate in riding the crest of a new revolutionary wave sweeping through the region. But if there are risks in a Sino-Vietnamese settlement, there are potential advantages as well, in the reduction of tension and the likelihood of a Great Power confrontation in the area. A period of peace and economic nation-building could be beneficial, not only to the peoples of the two countries themselves, but for the region and the rest of the world as well.

Selected Bibliography

Documents

Black Paper: Facts and Evidences of the Acts of Aggression and Annexation of Vietnam against Kampuchea. Democratic Kampuchea: Ministry of Foreign Affairs, 1978.

Chinese Aggression against Vietnam: Dossier. Hanoi, 1979.

"China's Indisputable Sovereignty over the Xisha and Nansha Islands." *Beijing Review,* February 18, 1980.

"CIA Secret Report on Sino-Vietnamese Reaction to American Tactics in the Vietnamese War." *Journal of Contemporary Asia,* vol. 13, no. 2 (1983).

Communist Vietnamese Publications. Microfilm Series issued by the Library of Congress, Washington, D.C.

"Document on Indochina Federation." *VNA,* April 17, 1978.

Lich su Dang Cong San Viet Nam: Trich van kien Dang [A history of the Vietnamese Communist party: selected party documents]. Hanoi, 1979.

"Memo on Vice-President Li Xiannian's Talks with Premier Pham Van Dong." *People's Daily,* March 23, 1979.

"Memorandum on Chinese Provocations and Territorial Encroachments upon Vietnamese Territory." *Vietnam News Bulletin,* April 10, 1979.

"On Hanoi's White Book." *Beijing Review,* November 23, 1979.

Policy of the People's Republic of Kampuchea with Regard to Vietnamese Residents." PRK: Ministry of Foreign Affairs, 1983.

"Report on the Situation on the Indochinese Peninsula." *Chung-kung yen-chiu* [Studies in Chinese communism]. Vol. 14, no. 10 (October 15, 1980). Translated in JPRS 77,074.

Some Evidence of the Plots Hatched by the Beijing Expansionists against the Kampuchean People. PRK: Ministry of Foreign Affairs, 1982.

The Chinese Rulers' Crimes against Kampuchea. PRK: Ministry of Foreign Affairs, April 1984.

"The Truth about Sino-Vietnamese Relations." *Guoji wenti yanjiu* [Studies in international problems], no. 2 (October 1981).

The Truth about Vietnamo-Chinese Relations over the Past Thirty Years. Hanoi: Ministry of Foreign Affairs, 1979.
Undeclared War against the People's Republic of Kampuchea. PRK: Ministry of Foreign Affairs, 1985.
"White Book on Vietnamese Archipelagoes." *VNA*, September 28, 1979.
Working Paper on North Vietnam's Role in the War in South Vietnam. Washington, D.C.: GPO, 1978. ???GPO???

Books

Armstrong, J. D. *Revolutionary Diplomacy: Chinese Foreign Policy and the United Front Doctrine.* Berkeley and Los Angeles: University of California Press, 1977.
Boudarel, Georges, et al., eds. *La Bureaucratie au Vietnam.* Paris: l'Harmattan, 1983.
Carter, Jimmy. *Keeping Faith: Memoirs of a President.* Toronto: Bantam Books, 1982.
Chandler, David P., and Kiernan, Ben. *Revolution and its Aftermath in Kampuchea: Eight Essays.* New Haven: Yale University Southeast Asia Studies, 1983.
Chen, King C. *China and the Three Worlds: A Foreign Policy Reader.* White Plains: M. E. Sharpe, 1979.
_____. *Vietnam and China, 1938–1954.* Princeton: Princeton University Press, 1969.
Chiang Yung-ching. *Hu Chih-ming tsai Chung-kuo* [Ho Chi Minh in China]. Taipei, 1972.
Deveria. G. *Histoire des Relations de la Chine avec l'Annam-Vietnam du XVIe au XIXe Siècle.* Paris: Ernest Leroux, 1980.
Duiker, William J. *The Comintern and Vietnamese Communism.* Athens: Ohio University Press, Center for International Studies, 1975.
_____. *The Communist Road to Power in Vietnam.* Boulder: Westview Press, 1981.
_____. *Vietnam since the Fall of Saigon.* Athens: Ohio University Monographs in International Studies, 1985.
Elliott, David W. P., ed. *The Third Indochina Conflict.* Boulder: Westview Press, 1981.
Etcheson, Craig. *The Rise and Demise of Democratic Kampuchea.* Boulder: Westview Press, 1984.
Fairbank, John K. *The Chinese World Order.* Cambridge: Harvard University Press, 1968.
Garver, John W. *China's Decision for Rapprochement with the United States, 1968–1971.* Boulder: Westview Press, 1982.
Gittings, John. *The World and China, 1922–1972.* New York: Harper and Row, 1974.

Gurtov, Melvin. *China and Southeast Asia: The Politics of Survival.* Baltimore: Johns Hopkins University Press, 1971.

———. *The First Indochina Crisis: Chinese Communist Strategy and United States Involvement, 1953-1954.* New York: Columbia University Press, 1967.

———, and Byong-moo Hwang. *China under Threat.* Baltimore: Johns Hopkins University Press, 1980.

Harrison, James Pinckney. *The Endless War: Fifty Years of Struggle in Vietnam.* New York: Free Press, 1982.

Hemery, Daniel. *Révolutionnaires Vietnamiens et pouvoir colonial en Indochine.* Paris: Maspero, 1975.

Heng Samrin. *La Révolution du Kampuchea est Irréversible.* PRK: Ministry of Foreign Affairs, 1984.

Hersh, Seymour M. *The Price of Power: Kissinger in the Nixon White House.* New York: Summit Books, 1983.

Hinton, Harold. *Turbulent Quest.* Bloomington: Indiana University Press, 1970.

Ho Chi Minh. *Selected Writings.* Hanoi: Foreign Languages Press, 1977.

Hun Sen. *La Solidarité Kampuchea-Vietnam.* Phnom Penh, 1982.

Huynh Kim Khanh. *Vietnamese Communism, 1925-1945.* Ithaca: Cornell University Press, 1982.

Joyaux, François. *La Chine et le Règlement du Premier Conflit d'Indochine (Genève 1954).* Paris: Sorbonne, 1979.

Kissinger, Henry. *White House Years.* Boston: Little, Brown, 1979.

Khrushchev, Nikita. *Khrushchev Remembers.* New York: Bantam, 1971.

Kuo T'ing-yi, ed. *Chung-yueh Wen-hua Lun-chi* [Essays on Sino-Vietnamese culture]. Taipei, 1956.

Lawson, Eugene K. *The Sino-Vietnamese Conflict.* New York: Praeger, 1984.

Levenson, Joseph. *Confucian China and Its Modern Fate.* Vol. 3. *The Problem of Intellectual Continuity.* London: Routledge and Kegan Paul, 1958.

Marr, David G. *Vietnamese Anticolonialism, 1885-1925.* Berkeley and Los Angeles: University of California Press, 1971.

———. *Vietnamese Tradition on Trial.* Berkeley and Los Angeles: University of California Press, 1981.

McLane, Charles B. *Soviet Strategies in Southeast Asia.* Princeton: Princeton University Press, 1966.

Moise, Edwin. *Land Reform in China and North Vietnam.* Chapel Hill: University of North Carolina Press, 1983.

Nguyen Khac Vien. *Tradition and Revolution in Vietnam.* Washington, D.C.: Indochina Resource Center, 1974.

Rousset, Pierre. *Communisme et nationalisme vietnamien.* Editions Galilée, 1978.

Sihanouk, Norodom. *War and Hope: The Case for Cambodia.* New York: Pantheon, 1980.
Smith, R. B. *An International History of the Vietnam War: Revolution vs. Containment, 1955–1961.* London: St. Martin's Press, 1983.
Smyser, W. R. *The Independent Vietnamese: Vietnamese Communism between Russia and China, 1956–1969.* Athens: Ohio University Press, Center for International Studies, 1980.
Suryadinata, Leo. *China and the ASEAN States: The Ethnic Chinese Dimension.* Kent Ridge: Singapore University Press, 1985.
Taylor, Jay. *China and Southeast Asia.* New York: Praeger, 1976.
Taylor, Keith. *The Birth of Vietnam.* Berkeley and Los Angeles: University of California Press, 1983.
Tran Huy Lieu. *Tai Lieu Tham Khao Lich Su Cach Mang Viet Nam* [Historical research materials concerning the modern revolution in Vietnam]. Hanoi, 1958.
Truong Chinh. *On Kampuchea.* Hanoi: Foreign Languages Press, 1980.
Truong Nhu Tang. *Vietcong Memoir: An Inside Account of the Revolution and Its Aftermath.* San Diego: Harcourt Brace Jovanovich, 1985.
Turley, William S., ed. *Confrontation or Coexistence: The Future of ASEAN-Vietnam Relations.* Bangkok: Institute of Security and International Studies, 1985.
———. *Interviews with PAVN and LDP Defectors: Officers, Men, and Political Cadres.* Carbondale: Southern Illinois Uniersity Press, 1974.
Van Ginneken, Jaap. *The Third Indochina War.* Leiden, 1983.
Vance, Cyrus. *Hard Choices: Critical Years in America's Foreign Policy.* New York: Simon and Schuster, 1983.
Vo Nguyen Giap. *Nhiem Vu Quan Su truc mat Chuyen Sang Tong Phan Cong* [The military task for preparing the counteroffensive]. Hanoi, 1950.
Woodside, Alexander B. *Community and Revolution in Vietnam.* Boston: Houghton Mifflin, 1976.
———. *Vietnam and the Chinese Model.* Cambridge: Harvard University Press, 1971.
Zagoria, Donald. *The Vietnam Triangle: Moscow, Peking, Hanoi.* New York: Pegasus, 1967.

Articles

Bekaert, Jacques. "Kampuchea's Loose Coalition: A Shotgun Wedding." *Indochina Issues,* no. 22 (December 1981).
Bui Nguyen. "Political work at places fighting encroachment and occupation by the enemy." *Tap chi Quan doi Nhan dan* [People's Army review], September 1982.

Boudarel, Georges. "Comment Giap a failli perdre la Bataille de Dien Bien Phu." *Le Nouvel Observateur,* April 8, 1983.

Chuong Thao. "Nguon goc chu nghia yeu nuoc cua Phan Boi Chau" [The origins of Phan Boi Chau's patriotism]. *Nghien Cuu Lich Su* [Historical research], no. 88 (July 1966).

Elliott, David W. P. "Institutionalizing the Revolution: Vietnam's Search for a Model of Development." In William S. Turley, ed., *Vietnamese Communism in Comparative Perspective.* Boulder: Westview Press, 1980.

Griffith, William E. "Sino-Soviet Rapprochement?" *Problems of Communism,* vol. 32 (March-April 1977).

Hiebert, Murray. "Cambodia and Vietnam: Costs of the Alliance." *Indochina Issues,* no. 46 (May 1984).

Hoang Tung, "The World Situation and the Foreign Policy of our Party and State." *Giao Duc Ly Luan* [Educational theory], no. 5 (September-October 1982). Translated in JPRS 82,735.

Kien Cuong. "Su phan boi cua nhung nguoi lanh dao Trung quoc tai Hoi nghi Gio-ne-vo nam 1954" [The Chinese leaders betrayal at the Geneva Conference of 1954]. *Nghien Cuu Lich Su* [Historical research], no. 184 (February 1980).

Nguyen Khac Vien. "Les specialistes du discours politique creux aux postes clefs et l'inflation bureaucratique." In Georges Boudarel et al., eds., *La Bureaucratie au Vietnam.* Paris: l'Harmattan, 1983.

Pham Hong Son. "The military thinking of Mao Zedong." *Tap Chi Cong San* [Communist review], no. 10 (October 1981).

Quinn-Judge, Paul. "China and Vietnam: Old Ties Remain." *Indochina Issues,* no. 53 (January 1985).

Porter, Gareth. "Hanoi's Strategic Perspective and the Sino-Vietnamese Conflict." *Pacific Affairs,* vol. 57, no. 1 (Spring 1984).

Rogers, Frank E. "Sino-Vietnamese Relations and the Vietnam War, 1965-1966." *China Quarterly,* no. 66 (April 1976).

Simon, Sheldon. "Peking and Indochina: The Perplexity of Victory." *Asian Survey,* May 1976.

Turley, William S., and Race, Jeffrey. "The Third Indochina War." *Foreign Policy,* no. 38 (Spring 1980).

van der Kroef, Justus. "The SOUTH CHINA SEA: Competing Claims and Strategic Conflicts." *International Security Review,* vol. 7, no. 3 (Fall 1982).

Van Tao. "Nhung net khac nhua giua cach mang Viet Nam va cach mang Trung quoc" [The differences between the Vietnamese and Chinese revolutions]. *Nghien Cuu Lich Su* [Historical research], no. 190 (January-February 1980).

Journals and Newspapers

Asian Survey
Beijing Review
China Quarterly
Christian Science Monitor
Far Eastern Economic Review
Guoji Wenti Yanjiu [Studies in international problems]
International Security Review
Los Angeles Times
Le Monde
Manchester Guardian
New York Times
Nghien Cuu Lich Su [Historical research]
Nhan Dan [The people]
Quan Doi Nhan Dan [People's Army]
Tap Chi Cong San [Communist review]
Vietnam Courier
Washington Post

Index

Angkor Empire, 5
ASEAN. *See* Association of Southeast Asian Nations
Association of Southeast Asian Nations (ASEAN), 81, 88, 95–115 passim
August Revolution, 16
Australia, 108

Bandung Conference, 52
Border dispute, 36–37, 61, 116
Brezhnev, Leonid, 47
Brzezinski, Zbigniew, 91fn.

Cam Ranh Bay, 123
Cambodia (*See also* Democratic Kampuchea, People's Republic of Kampuchea), 23, 26, 28–32, 35, 51–60
Carter, Jimmy, 85
Champa, 5
Chen I (Ch'en Yi), 46
Chernenko, Konstantin, 111
Chiang Kai-shek, 10–11, 13, 18, 38
China (*See also* People's Republic of China), expansion to the south, 3–4, 6; influence on Vietnam, 3–6, 10
Chinese Communist Party (CCP), 12–15, 18, 70, 98–99, 106; factions in, 48–49, 56, 82–83
Chu Van Tan, 72
CMEA. *See* Council for Mutual Economic Assistance

Coalition Government of Democratic Kampuchea (CGDK), 100–115 passim, 119
Cold War, viii, 23, 31, 91
Comintern, 11–14, 29
Confucianism, 4, 5fn., 6–11
Council for Mutual Economic Assistance (CMEA), 65, 77, 123

Dai Viet, 4
Democratic Kampuchea, 65–70, 80–84, 93, 95–115 passim; factions in, 68, 70, 80
Democratic Republic of Vietnam (DRV), 16, 19, 24; founded, 16; foreign policy at Geneva Conference, 24–32; relations with Cambodia, 28–32, 51–58, 60, 65–67, 73–74; relations with Laos, 28–32; relations with the United States, 26
Deng Xiaoping (Teng Hsiao-p'ing), 45, 48, 64, 72, 77–78, 81–82, 84–86, 98, 107, 111, 113fn.
Deng Yingzhao (Teng Ying-chao), 76
Dien Bien Phu, Battle of, 22–23, 25, 32–33
Dulles, John Foster, 24

Easter Offensive, 59

France, 36; conquest of Vietnam, 8; colonial policy, 10–11, 16–17; occupation of Paracels and Spratlys, 38–39; loses control over Vietnam, 16–20, 24–25
French Communist Party, 17
FUNK. *See* National United Front of Kampuchea

Gang of Four, 82
Geneva Conference, 21–37, 41–42, 55
Government of Vietnam (also known as South Vietnam), 42, 44–45
Great Proletarian Cultural Revolution, 107, 116
Gulf of Thailand, 66 70
Guomindang (Kuomintang), 10, 12

Han dynasty, 3
Heng Samrin, 80, 84
Ho Chi Minh, vii, 12, 13–19, 21, 24–26, 29–31, 33, 40, 50fn., 118fn.
Hoang Van Hoan, 25fn., 26fn., 71
Hu Yaobang (Hu Yao-pang), 111
Huang Hua, 68, 69fn., 73fn.

ICP. *See* Indochinese Communist Party
Ieng Sary, 78, 98, 112
India, 30–31
Indochina Summit Conference (1970), 57

Indochinese Communist Party (ICP), 13–15, 17, 20, 28–29, 32
Indochinese Federation, 29, 30fn, 31, 36, 65, 69
Indonesia, 91fn., 99, 108, 116

Japan, 15–16, 38–39
Jiang Qing (Chiang Ch'ing), 64fn
Johnson, Lyndon, 47fn.
Joyaux, Francois, 30

Kampuchea. *See* Cambodia
Kampuchean Communist Party (KCP), 53–55, 60, 95
Kampuchean National United Front for National Salvation (KNUFNS), 80
Kampuchean People's Revolutionary Party (KPRP), 30, 52–53, 95, 115
Kang Youwei (K'ang Yu-wei), 8
KCP. *See* Kampuchean Communist Party
Khieu Samphan, 55fn., 68fn.
Khmer Rouge, 54–55, 60, 83, 88, 96–99, 103, 110, 112
Khrushchev, Nikita, 25fn., 26fn., 33, 42–44, 47
Kissinger, Henry, 53, 59
KNUFNS. *See* Kampuchean National United Front for National Salvation
Korean War, 23–24, 32
KPRP. *See* Kampuchean People's Revolutionary Party

Lac peoples, 2–4
Lang Son, Battle of, 87–88

Laniel, Joseph, 25
Lao People's Revolutionary party (LPRP), 30
Laos, 23, 26, 28, 32, 35, 65, 100, 106, 113fn.
Le Duan, 49–51, 59, 63–66, 69, 72, 112
Le Duc Tho, 51fn., 54fn.
Le Loi, 6
Le Quang Ba, 72
Le Thanh Nghi, 63
Le Thanh Tong, 6
Lenin, Vladimir, 63
Liang Qichao (Liang Ch'i-ch'ao), 8
Lin Biao (Lin Piao), 48–49
Liu Shaoqi (Liu Shao-ch'i), 19, 44, 48
Lo Guibo (Lo Kuei-po), 20
Lon Nol, 53–54, 56 LPRP. *See* Lao People's Revolutionary Party

Malaysia, 99, 111, 116
Mao Zedong (Mao Tse-tung), 13, 19, 33, 40, 43, 47–48, 60, 63, 106–107
Maoism, 106
Maoist model, 15, 19–22, 40–41, 123
Maozedong Thought, 72, 106, 116
Marxism-Leninism, 11, 18–19, 21, 28, 106–107
May Fourth Movement, 10
Ming dynasty, 6

National United Front for Kampuchea (FUNK), 56
Nehru, Jawaharlal, 30–31

Ngo Dinh Diem, 42–45
Nguyen Co Thach, 80, 97
Nguyen dynasty, 7
Nguyen Trai, 6–7
Nixon, Richard, 58–59

Pak Mai (New Party), 103fn
Paracel Islands, 37–39, 61, 72–73
PAVN. *See* People's Army of Vietnam
Pen Sovan, 115fn.
People's Army of Vietnam (PAVN), 22, 72, 80, 82, 85–87, 109, 111, 114
People's Liberation Army (PLA), 85–87
People's Republic of Kampuchea (PRK), 83, 95–115 passim, 119
People's Republic of China (PRC), aid to Vietnam, 17–27, 35, 41, 43–50, 60, 63–64, 75, 77; foreign policy objectives, 18–19, 23–25, 27, 43–44, 49, 82–83, 99, 101–102, 111, 116–122; invasion of Vietnam (1979), 83–89; policy toward overseas Chinese, 39–40, 71, 74–77, 89–90, 116; relations with ASEAN states, 81, 88, 99–115 passim, 119, 124–125; relations with Cambodia, 28–31, 51–57, 60, 65–71, 73–74, 80–81, 89–90, 95–115 passim; relations with Laos, 28–31, 100; relations with the Soviet Union, 47–49, 56, 65, 67–69, 82, 84, 91, 101, 109, 111, 113–114, 120; relations with the United States, 23–27, 35, 43, 46–47, 50, 56, 58–59, 82, 84, 99, 111; strategic advice

to Vietnam, 43–44, 46, 49–50, 90
People's War. *See* Maoist model
People's Army of Vietnam (PAVN), 22, 72, 80, 82, 85–87, 109, 111, 114
Pham Van Dong, 33, 39, 51fn., 55–56, 59–60, 72, 79
Phan Boi Chau, 8–9, 21
Phan Chu Trinh, 8, 9fn.
Phan Khoi, 10
Philippines, 104
PLA. *See* People's Liberation Army
Pol Pot (Saloth Sar), 53–55, 60, 66–71, 73–81, 99, 112
PRC. *See* People's Republic of China
PRK. *See* People's Republic of Kampuchea
Proximity talks, 111–112

Qin (Ch'in) dynasty, 3
Qing (Ch'ing) dynasty, 8, 18, 36
Quoc ngu, 11

Refugees, 75–77, 89–90

Sainteny, Jean, 16
Sea boundary, 37, 61
SEATO. *See* Southeast Asia Treaty Organization
Sihanouk, Norodom, 51–57, 60, 67, 98–100, 103
So Phim, 70, 74, 77
Socialist Republic of Vietnam (SRV), foreign policy objectives, 95–115 passim, 122–125; internal situation, 71, 74, 77–78, 106; invasion of Democratic Kampuchea, 74, 77–84; relations with ASEAN states, 79, 95–115 passim, 119–120; relations with Kampuchea, 77–84, 93, 95–115 passim; relations with the United States, 79–80, 108–109, 120
Son Sann, 100, 103
Son Sen, 78
Soong Qingling (Sung Ch'ing-ling), 13fn.
South China Sea, 37–39, 72, 100
Southeast Asia Treaty Organization (SEATO), 35
Souvanna Phouma, 65
Soviet Union (USSR), 14–15, 18, 23; aid to Vietnam, 41, 44, 47–48, 64, 78–79, 86, 113–114; policy toward Vietnam, 12–13, 17, 25, 28, 32, 35, 42, 44, 46, 59, 65, 79, 86, 91–93, 101, 113–114, 121, 124; Treaty of Friendship and Cooperation with Vietnam, 79–80, 84, 86, 92, 119
Special relations, 65–66, 93–94, 101–103, 114, 119–120
Spratly Islands, 37–39, 72–73, 100
SRV. *See* Socialist Republic of Vietnam
Stalin, Joseph, 27
Stalin School, 12–14
Sun Yat-sen, 9–10, 12, 13fn., 21

Taiwan, 43, 60
Taylor, Jay, 124
Thai Communist Party (TCP), 99, 103
Thailand, 52, 95, 97, 99, 106, 109, 113

135

Three Worlds Theory, 64, 67
Tong (T'ang) dynasty, 4
Tonkin Gulf, 36–37, 60–61, 73, 100
Tonkin Gulf Incident, 47
Tran Trong Kim, 10
Tributary relationship, 1, 4–5, 8, 90
Truong Chinh, 51fn.

United States, 18, 23–24, 32, 35, 42, 44, 47, 57, 82, 84–85, 91–93, 109–110, 124

Van Lang, 2–4
VCP. *See* Vietnamese Communist Party
Vietminh, 15fn., 16–17, 19–20, 22–25, 29, 32–33, 90–91
Vietnam Quoc Dan Dang (VNQDD), 10
Vietnam War, vii, 42–51
Vietnamese, origins of, 1–2; national consciousness, 4–11
Vietnamese Communist Party (VCP), 76; origins, 12–13; factions, 71, 78, 106; Fourth National Congress, 71; Fourth Plenum, 71, 77; Fifth Plenum, 78–79; Seventh Plenum, 109
Vietnamese Revolutionary Youth League, 11–13 Vietnamese Workers' Party (VWP), 20–21; factions, 45; Second National Congress, 29
Vo Dong Giang, 80, 118–120
Vo Nguyen Giap, 51fn.
VWP. *See* Vietnamese Workers' Party

Wei Guoqing (Wei Kuo-ching), 19
Whampoa Academy, 12
Wu Xueqian (Wu Hsueh-ch'ien), 100

Zhang Faguei (Chang Fa-quei), 16
Zheng Geng (Cheng Keng), 19
Zhou Enlai (Chou En-lai), 23, 25–28, 30–31, 39–40, 52, 63, 68fn., 70, 72

INSTITUTE OF EAST ASIAN STUDIES PUBLICATIONS SERIES

CHINA RESEARCH MONOGRAPHS (CRM)

6. David D. Barrett. *Dixie Mission: The United States Army Observer Group in Yenan, 1944,* 1970 ($4.00)
15. Joyce K. Kallgren, Editor. *The People's Republic of China after Thirty Years: An Overview,* 1979 ($5.00)
16. Tong-eng Wang. *Economic Policies and Price Stability in China,* 1980 ($8.00)
17. Frederic Wakeman, Jr., Editor. *Ming and Qing Historical Studies in the People's Republic of China,* 1981 ($10.00)
18. Robert E. Bedeski. *State-Building in Modern China: The Kuomintang in the Prewar Period,* 1981 ($8.00)
19. Stanley Rosen. *The Role of Sent-Down Youth in the Chinese Cultural Revolution: The Case of Guangzhou,* 1981 ($8.00)
21. James H. Cole. *The People Versus the Taipings: Bao Lisheng's "Righteous Army of Dongan,"* 1981 ($7.00)
22. Dan C. Sanford. *The Future Association of Taiwan with the People's Republic of China,* 1982 ($8.00)
23. A. James Gregor with Maria Hsia Chang and Andrew B. Zimmerman. *Ideology and Development: Sun Yat-sen and the Economic History of Taiwan,* 1982 ($8.00)
24. Pao-min Chang. *Beijing, Hanoi, and the Overseas Chinese,* 1982 ($7.00)
25. Rudolf G. Wagner. *Reenacting the Heavenly Vision: The Role of Religion in the Taiping Rebellion,* 1984 ($12.00)
26. Patricia Stranahan. *Yan'an Women and the Communist Party,* 1984 ($12.00)
sp. Lucie Cheng, Charlotte Furth, and Hon-ming Yip, Editors. *Women in China: Bibliography of Available English Language Materials,* 1984 ($12.00)
27. John N. Hart. *The Making of an Army "Old China Hand": A Memoir of Colonel David D. Barrett,* 1985 ($12.00)
28. Steven A. Leibo. *Transferring Technology to China: Prosper Giquel and the Self-strengthening Movement,* 1985 ($15.00)
29. David Bachman. *Chen Yun and the Chinese Political System,* 1985 ($15.00)
30. Maria Hsia Chang. *The Chinese Blue Shirt Society: Fascism and Developmental Nationalism,* 1985 ($15.00)
31. Robert Y. Eng. *Economic Imperialism in China: Silk Production and Exports, 1861–1932,* 1986 ($15.00)

KOREA RESEARCH MONOGRAPHS (KRM)

5. William Shaw. *Legal Norms in a Confucian State,* 1981 ($10.00)
6. Youngil Lim. *Government Policy and Private Enterprise: Korean Experience in Industrialization,* 1982 ($8.00)
7. Q. Y. Kim. *The Fall of Syngman Rhee,* 1983 ($12.00)
8. Robert A. Scalapino and Jun-yop Kim, Editors. *North Korea Today: Strategic and Domestic Issues,* 1983 ($20.00)
9. Helen Hardacre. *The Religion of Japan's Korean Minority: The Preservation of Ethnic Identity,* 1985 ($12.00)
10. Fred C. Bohm and Robert R. Swartout, Jr., Editors. *Naval Surgeon in Yi Korea: The Journal of George W. Woods,* 1984 ($12.00)
11. Robert A. Scalapino and Hongkoo Lee, Editors. *North Korea in a Regional and Global Context,* 1986 ($20.00)
12. Laurel Kendall and Griffin Dix, Editors. *Religion and Ritual in Korean Society,* Winter 1986 ($ TBA)

JAPAN RESEARCH MONOGRAPHS (JRM)

2. James W. White. *Migration in Metropolitan Japan: Social Change and Political Behavior,* 1983 ($12.00)
3. James Cahill. *Sakaki Hyakusen and Early Nanga Painting,* 1983 ($10.00)